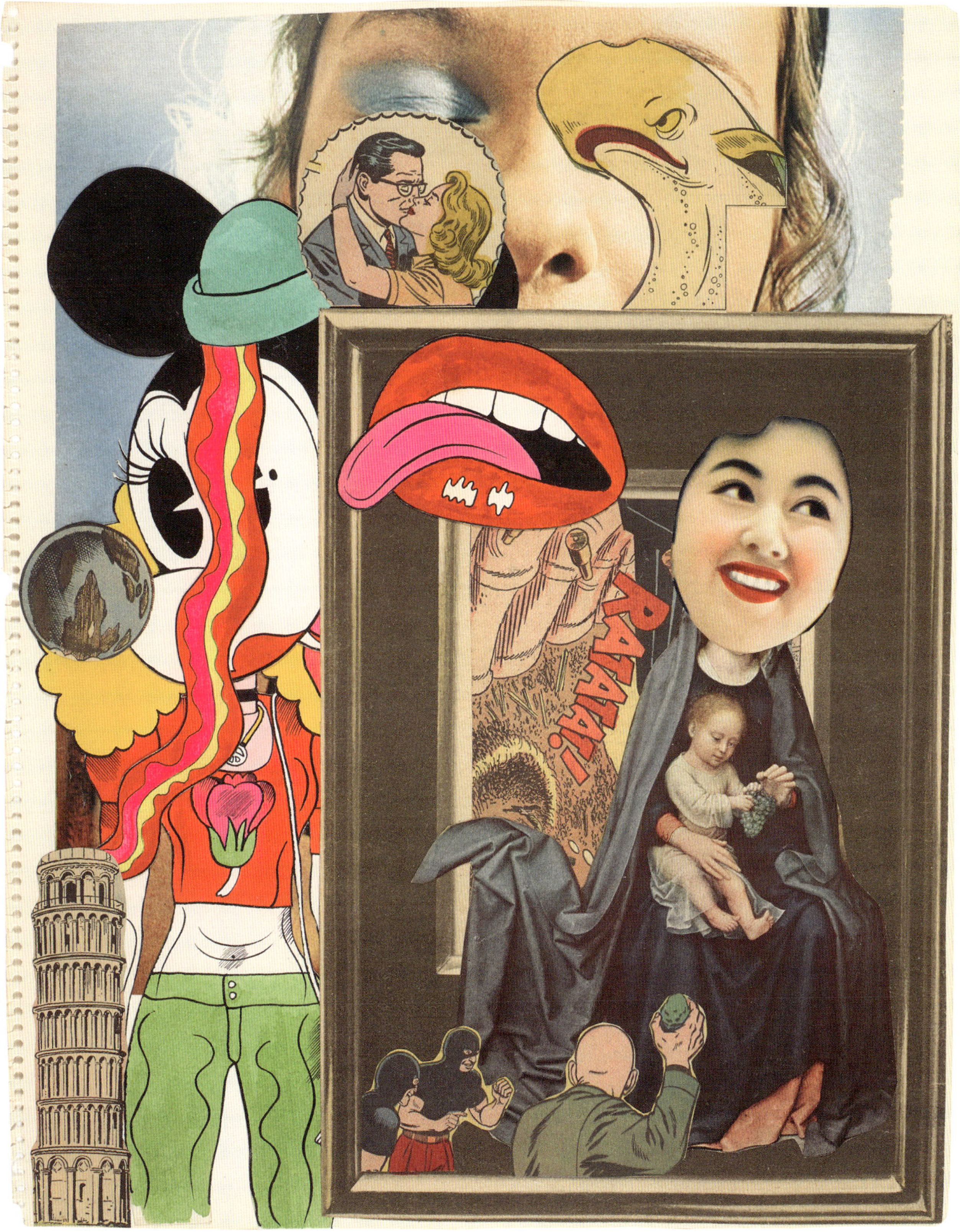

AF477459

Keiichi Tanaami
Collage as Resublimation

BY **TOM MCDONOUGH**

Keiichi Tanaami is justly celebrated as a Japanese pioneer of animation, capturing his ecstatically psychedelic visions of American mass-cultural icons in short films like *Good-by Elvis and USA* (1971) and *Good-by Marilyn* (1971). Combining his hand drawing with photographs from advertising, pornography, and film, he created a hallucinatory iconography of erotic and frequently grotesque import: hot dogs, the Empire State Building, blonde and buxom American women, bunny superheroes, mushrooms, the Statue of Liberty, airplanes, muscle men, bananas. Here, Tanaami's drawing echoes Milton Glaser's iconic 1966 poster of Bob Dylan, or Peter Max (then at the height of his fame) and with at least a passing resemblance to the animation found in *Yellow Submarine* (1968). Such foreign influences are filtered through a sensibility formed by the bold mid-sixties graphic designs of Yokoo Tadanori. These films, in their style and subjects, bear the traces of Tanaami's first visit to New York, in 1969, where he encountered the underground scene—in cinema, with Kenneth Anger, Jonas Mekas, and Andy Warhol, and in comics, with Robert Crumb. The pervasive sexuality of Tanaami's animated work derives less from a counterculture of free love than from a generalized desublimation fueling the American commodity economy, a tendency that registered in all its ambivalence within the contemporary productions of Pop art. Unsurprisingly, some of Tom Wesselmann's least subtle works—including his *Smoker, 1 (Mouth, 12)* (1967), which had just entered the collection of the Museum of Modern Art when Tanaami arrived in New York—appear fleetingly in the Japanese artist's homage to Marilyn Monroe.

Some of that same iconography appears in a small group of collages he made in 1969, perhaps while still in New York. Here too we find the Statue of Liberty, the American flag, nude bodies, superheroes, and soft drinks. In works such as *Coca-Cola and Flag* and *Burned Letter*, however, the overt eroticism of Tanaami's animations is tempered by a paratactic survey of the contradictions of American cultural life. Some of his source material is immediately recognizable as

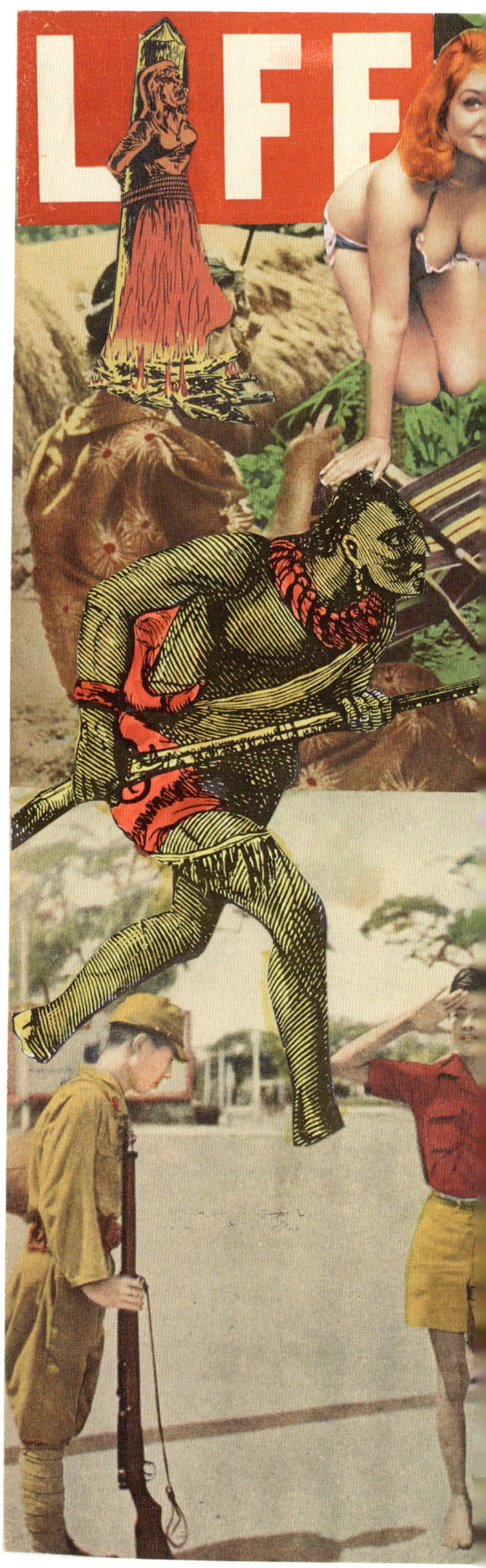

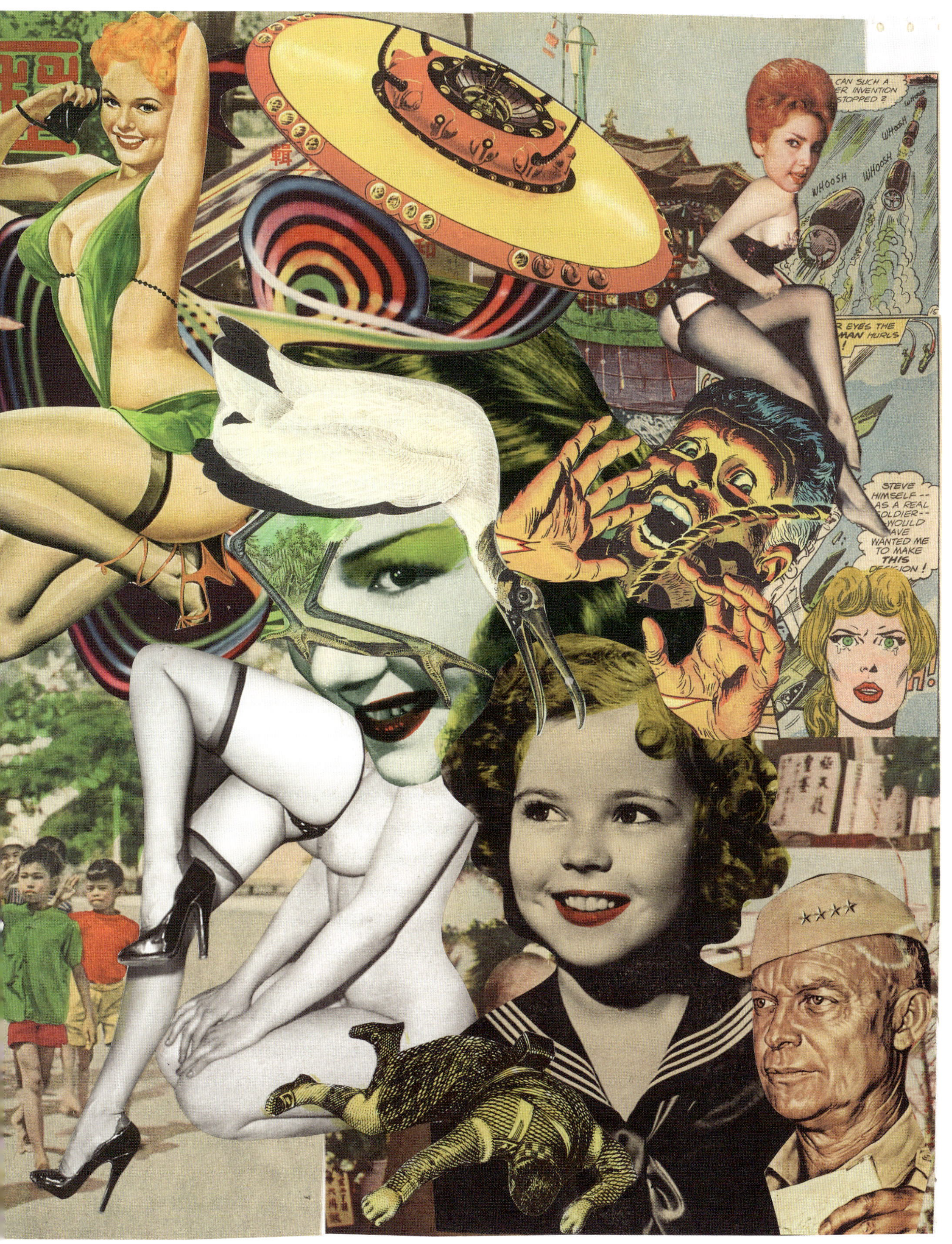
CAN SUCH A
ER INVENTION
STOPPED ?
WHOOSH
WHOOSH
WHOOSH
WHOOSH
R EYES THE
MAN HURLS
STEVE
HIMSELF --
AS A REAL
SOLDIER --
WOULD
HAVE
WANTED ME
TO MAKE
THIS
DECISION !

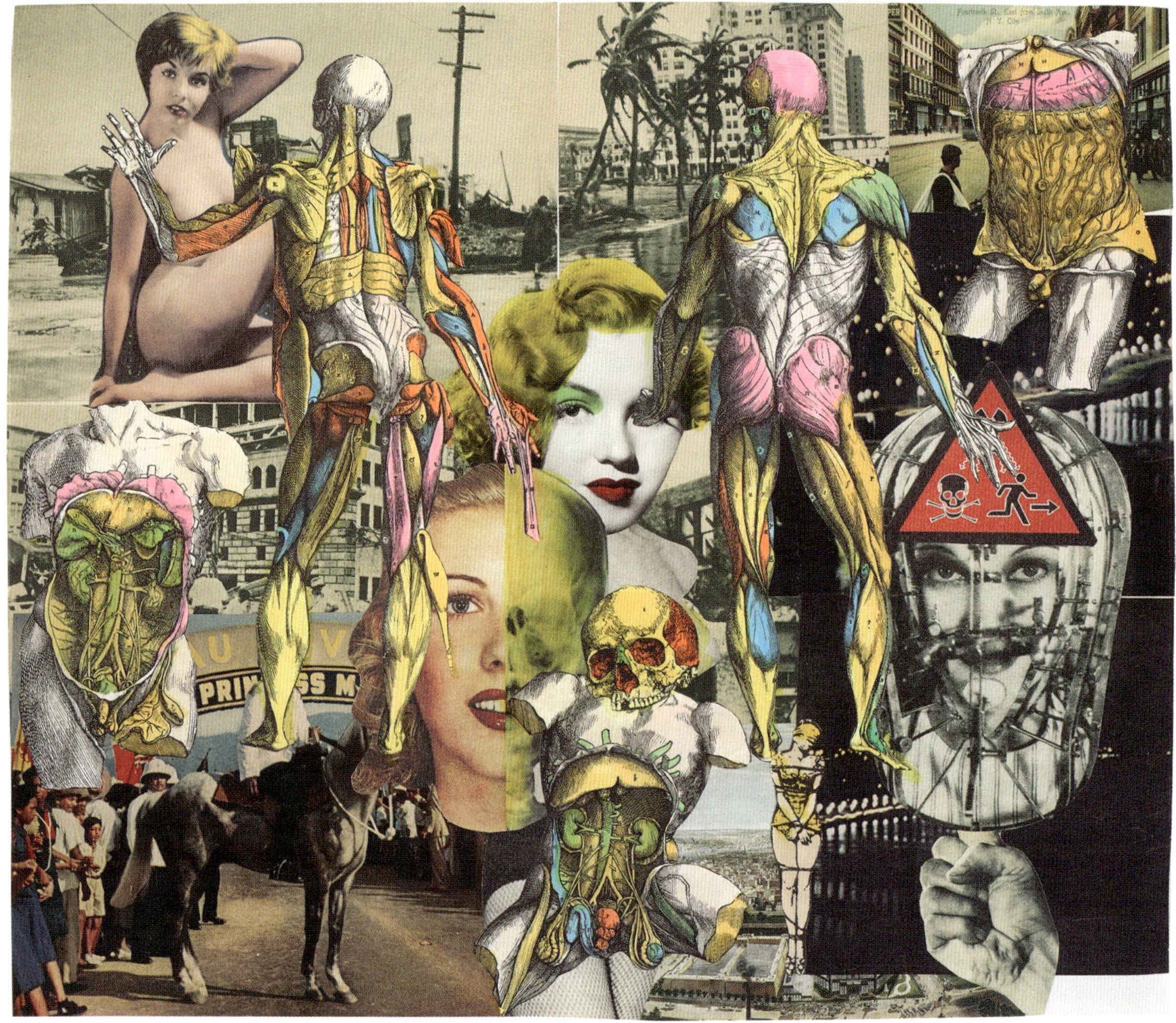

Collage Book 7_50 (1970)

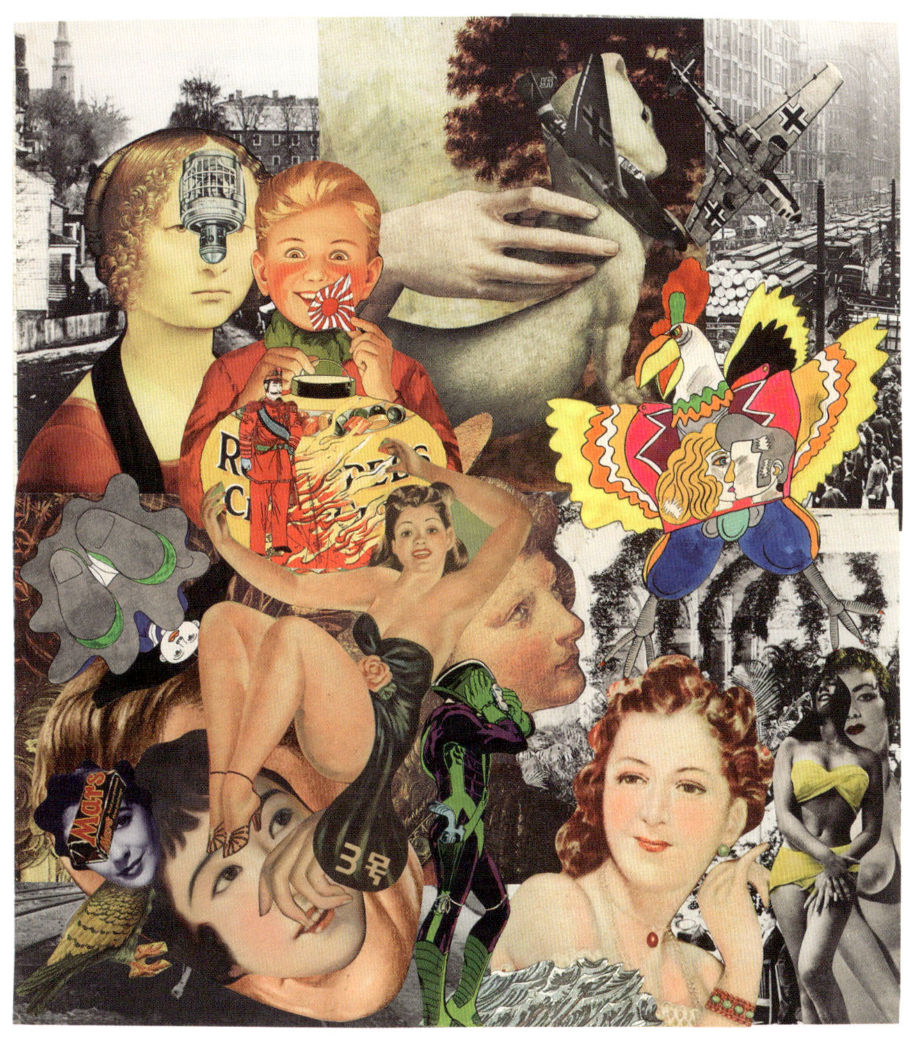

Collage Book 9_10 (1971)

iconic imagery of this turbulent moment: the David Montgomery photograph of a harem of naked women that graced the cover of the English release of Jimi Hendrix's 1968 *Electric Ladyland* album; or a detail from *Ramparts* magazine's infamous December 1967 cover, a photograph of hands holding the burning draft cards of its four editors. Certainly sex remains evident in these works. *Burned Letter* includes a collaged cartoon by Tanaami of a provocatively posed woman, clad only in stockings, with the head of Mickey Mouse, derived from his contemporaneous 42nd Street drawing cycle—but it is subsumed within a more general response to the overwhelming shock of mass-cultural forms that were simultaneously liberating desire and chaining it to the commodity, with this dynamic seen against the backdrop of the violence of imperialist war abroad and brutal repression of subaltern populations at home.

More remarkable are the photographic collages Tanaami produced after this trip to America, works that he only rediscovered in 2012 as he was, in his words, "tidying up at a warehouse in Setagaya," a neighborhood in southwest Tokyo. There he came across "a large stack of paper wrapped in old newspaper," what turned out to be dozens of forgotten photomontages known collectively as the Collage Books, broadly dated 1969–1975. For Tanaami, their rediscovery was profoundly troubling, even uncanny: "I had no memory of these dusty old newspapers," he has written. "I had no idea as to how, when, or for what reason this group of works had been made, and though these were unmistakably works of my own, for a moment I could not even fathom why they would have lain dormant here, abandoned in a dark warehouse." The disavowal expressed in these words is clear, yet upon examining the collages back in his studio, Tanaami experienced a flood of recollections, a veritable return of the repressed— "distant, blurry memories" that "came back to me, resurrected in vivid colors and stirring up strange emotions. As I looked at several of the photographs glued onto the background of one collage, a range of scenes I had completely forgotten about emerged."

Those memories were of Tanaami's childhood during and immediately following World War II, when at the age of six his family had relocated from their home in Kyōbashi in central Tokyo, under direct threat of American bombing, to a more distant ward to live with the artist's grandfather. Ultimately he and his mother would seek increased safety in the city of Niigata, on the west coast of the country— ironically, since this major port was one of the initial targets selected by the Americans for the atomic bomb—only returning to the ruins of Tokyo at the end of the war. What he found there, in his grandfather's house, was a trove of old printed materials dating from the 1930s left behind by an uncle who had subsequently been killed while serving in the Japanese army, an "enormous, breathing collection of magazines and picture postcards … like a mountain of treasures," kept in a closet. Perusing these forbidden materials became "a secret pastime" of Tanaami's adolescence—doubly forbidden, we might say, since the library consisted, on one hand, of propaganda materials from years of the discredited Tripartite Pact and, on the other, of movie magazines featuring the alluring faces and bodies of Hollywood stars. In the oppressive climate of the immediate postwar years, a time of abnegation and conservatism under the American occupying forces, this secret trove conjoined the politically and the sexually illicit.

Some twenty-five years later, Tanaami revisited that discovery in the closet of the house in Meguro. Now in his early thirties, a successful illustrator and graphic designer who had long been close to the Neo Dada artists Shinohara Ushio and Miki Tomio, he undertook a vast project that brought these two forbidden obsessions together in his *Collage Books*, whose private production seems to have occupied the artist for almost half a decade at the opening of the 1970s. Photos of smiling stars from movie magazines jostle with tinted postcards of Japanese soldiers, romance and war comics abut images of Renaissance masterpieces, pin-ups and anatomical drawings compete for our attention. Sometimes Tanaami's own hand is evident, as in a cartoonish mouth, moist lips parted and tongue dangling—another nod to Wesselmann, no doubt—found in *Collage Book 1_07*. In *Collage Book 7_13*, the contrasting force of a postcard showing a group of young boys saluting a Japanese soldier as they pass and a studio portrait of Shirley Temple in a sailor suit—her lips and hair tinted in the gaudy tones of Warhol's *Marilyns*—anchors the composition, which is generally structured around the opposition of (largely unclothed) female bodies and wartime scenes (taken from older engravings or more recent American war comics). That observation holds generally true for the series, but is nowhere as forcefully declared as in *Collage Book 7_50*, where femininity is dissected by the "beauty micrometer" and by X-ray, while flayed and dissected masculine bodies from Andreas Vesalius's sixteenth-century *De corporis humani* court an array of comely female flesh. These *vanitas* themes are set against historical postcards, one at the upper right of West 14th Street in New York, others of more devastated urban settings, although whether the damage is from natural or human forces remains unclear.

Tanaami is normally thought of a protagonist of Japanese Pop, and indeed the influence of Warhol and Wesselmann is apparent in these works. But something darker than Pop lurks in the *Collage Books*. The artist has mentioned the significance of Max Ernst for his photomontage practice, describing the impact of seeing a "mysterious, mystical collage, composed of illustrations from popular novels and mechanical parts catalogues and pictorial plates from science magazines." Although his sources would differ, Tanaami similarly mined a treasury of obsolete printed materials to revisit the traumas of his childhood, displacing his bourgeois, textile-merchant father with the prohibited legacy of his uncle, killed in the war so many were desperately trying to forget in Japan's precipitous reconstruction. Something in the traumatic, ecstatic encounter with American mass culture during his 1969 trip triggered those recollections and spurred him to pick up scissors and glue upon his return to Tokyo; the uncle's hoard was disassembled and reassembled into this vast atlas of sex and death. We can only imagine that its rediscovery over thirty years later was similarly conditioned by trauma—the 2012 visit to the Setagaya warehouse was prepared, on one side, by the Japanese earthquake and tsunami of the preceding year with its vast destruction and, on the other, by the reelection of Shinzō Abe at the end of the year, whose rightwing nationalist views have once again brought the wartime years into the headlines. Whatever the private and public preconditions for their reappearance, we're fortunate to have the *Collage Books* with us once again, a testament to Tanaami's remarkable, delirious view of our image world.

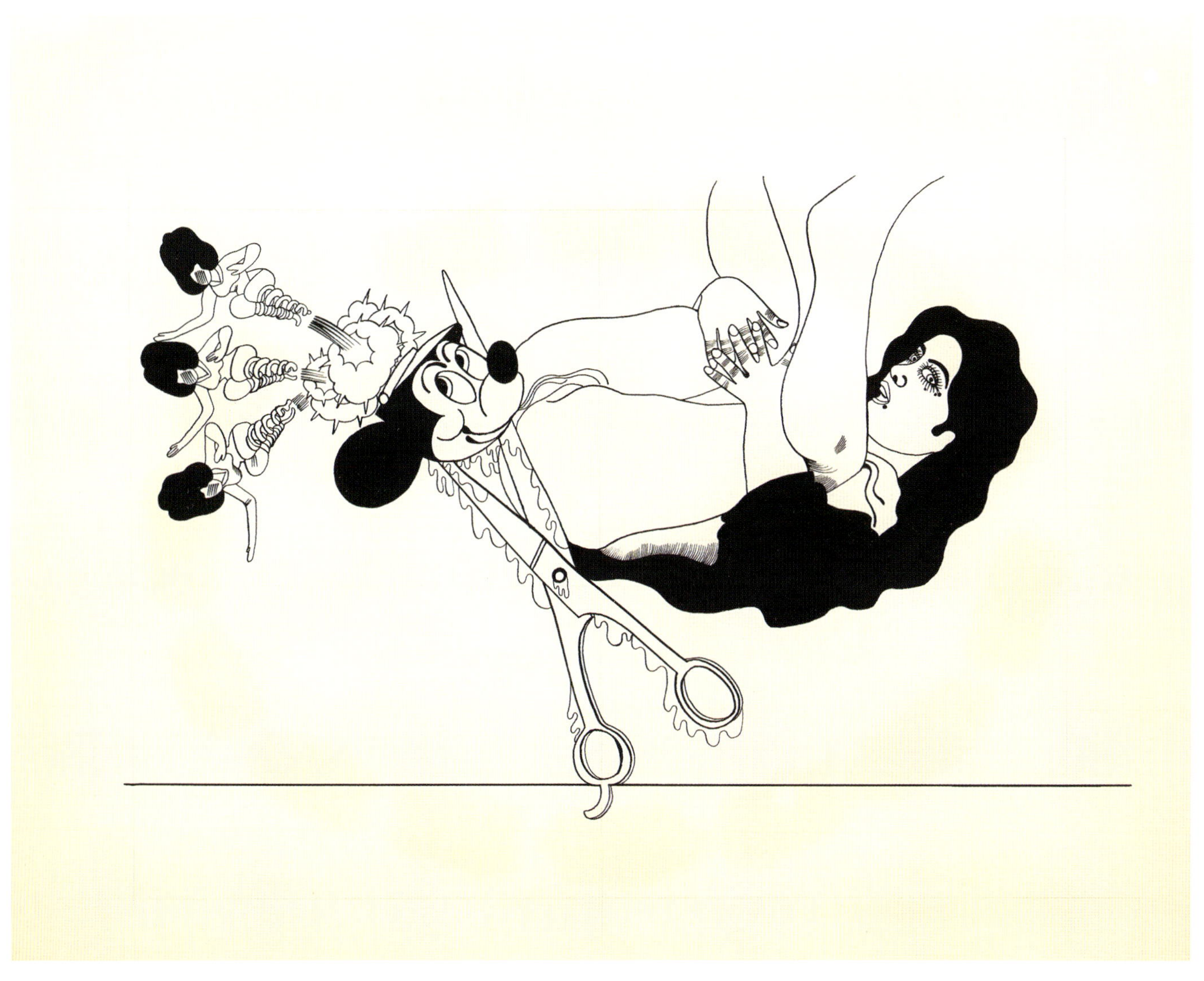

42nd Street Scissors (1969)

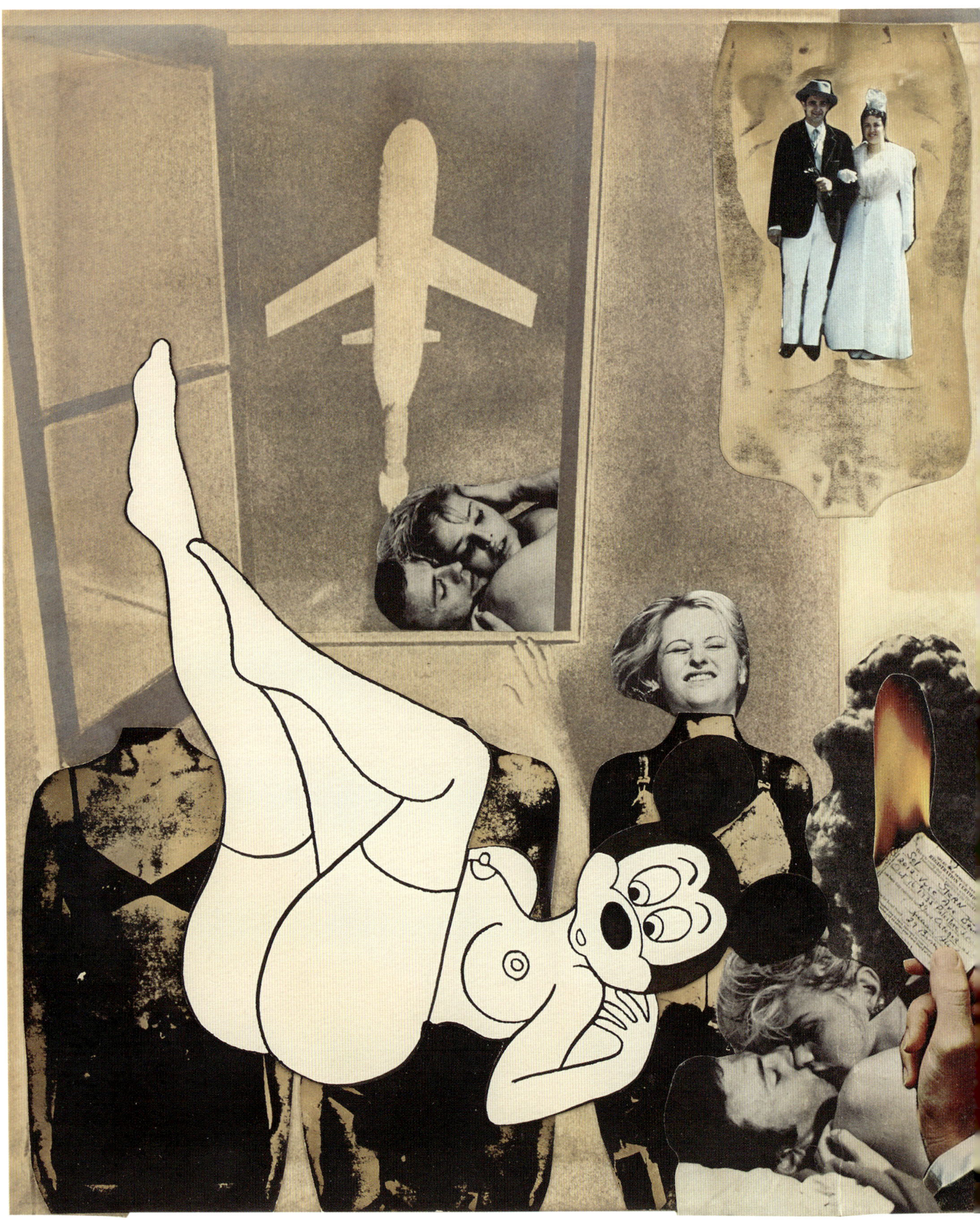

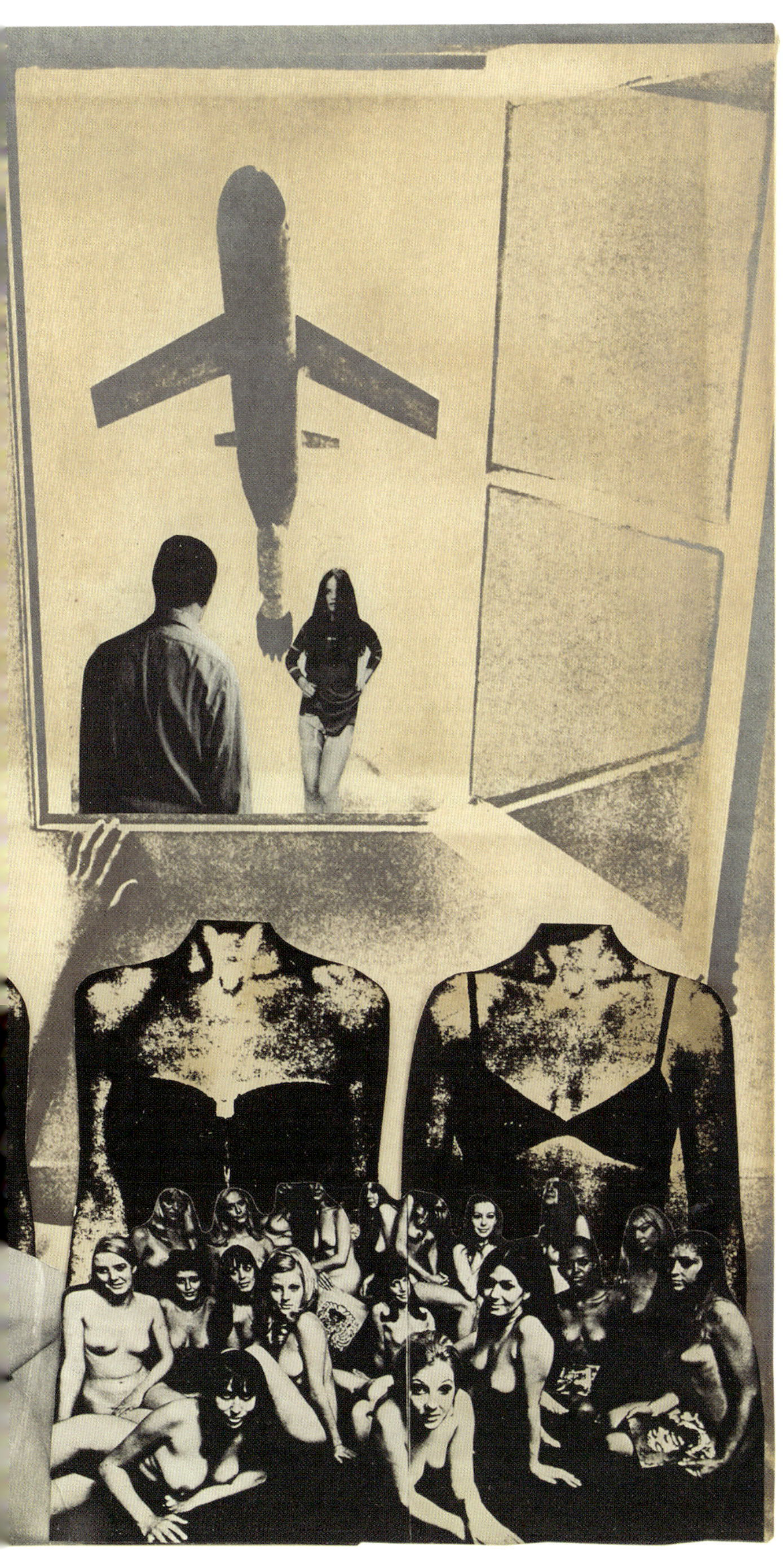

HORSE POWER

BY **ANN MARIE PEÑA**

Since entering the contemporary art world's consciousness a decade ago with a powerful series of staged images depicting youths in Paris' suburbs, Mohamed Bourouissa has become known for making work that shatters and disturbs our view of life within (and just outside of) the margins of urbanity. This early series of photographs titled Périphérique (2007–08) presents the oft-misrepresented youth culture of these outer districts, in which Bourouissa himself grew up, with an insider's gaze and understanding. When the photographs were first exhibited they seemed to evoke a new kind of raw consciousness of the present tense, to move beyond clichéd representations of black and Arab teenagers marginalized from France's middle-class establishment.

The photographs in Périphérique were staged with an exceptional intelligence that touched on allegory and art history, while also presenting a clear and taut visual language. It was no surprise that Bourouissa went on to be featured in key exhibitions such as the New Museum's 2009 inaugural triennial *Younger Than Jesus* and later the Prix Pictet.

Bourouissa has continued to develop in his role as a practitioner who plays within the duality of being the outsider on the inside, and vice versa. He can easily be defined as a photographer and filmmaker, but in reality Bourouissa's true practice seems to lie more in realm of method actor, so deep is his commitment and assimilation into the context in which he is working. In the series Temps Mort (2009), for which he (illicitly) gave an incarcerated acquaintance a mobile telephone to take photographs of his daily life in prison, there seems to be a tenacity to give what curator Adelina Vlas has described as "a sense of humanity to a marginal condition frequently unnoticed." For Temps Mort Bourouissa instructed his collaborator by text message to show what life was like on the inside, asking him to take pictures of things as simple as the view of the window from a particular position

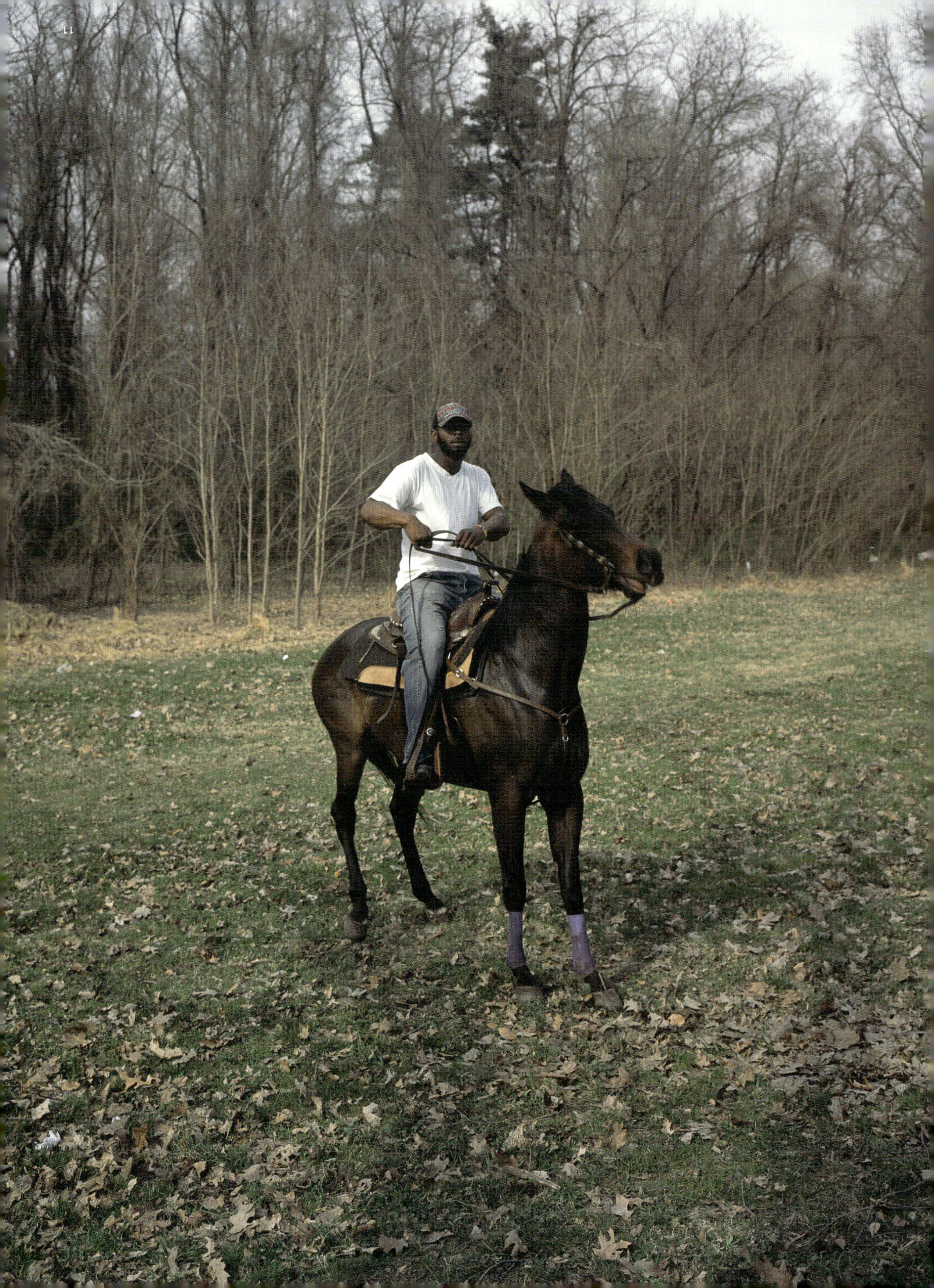

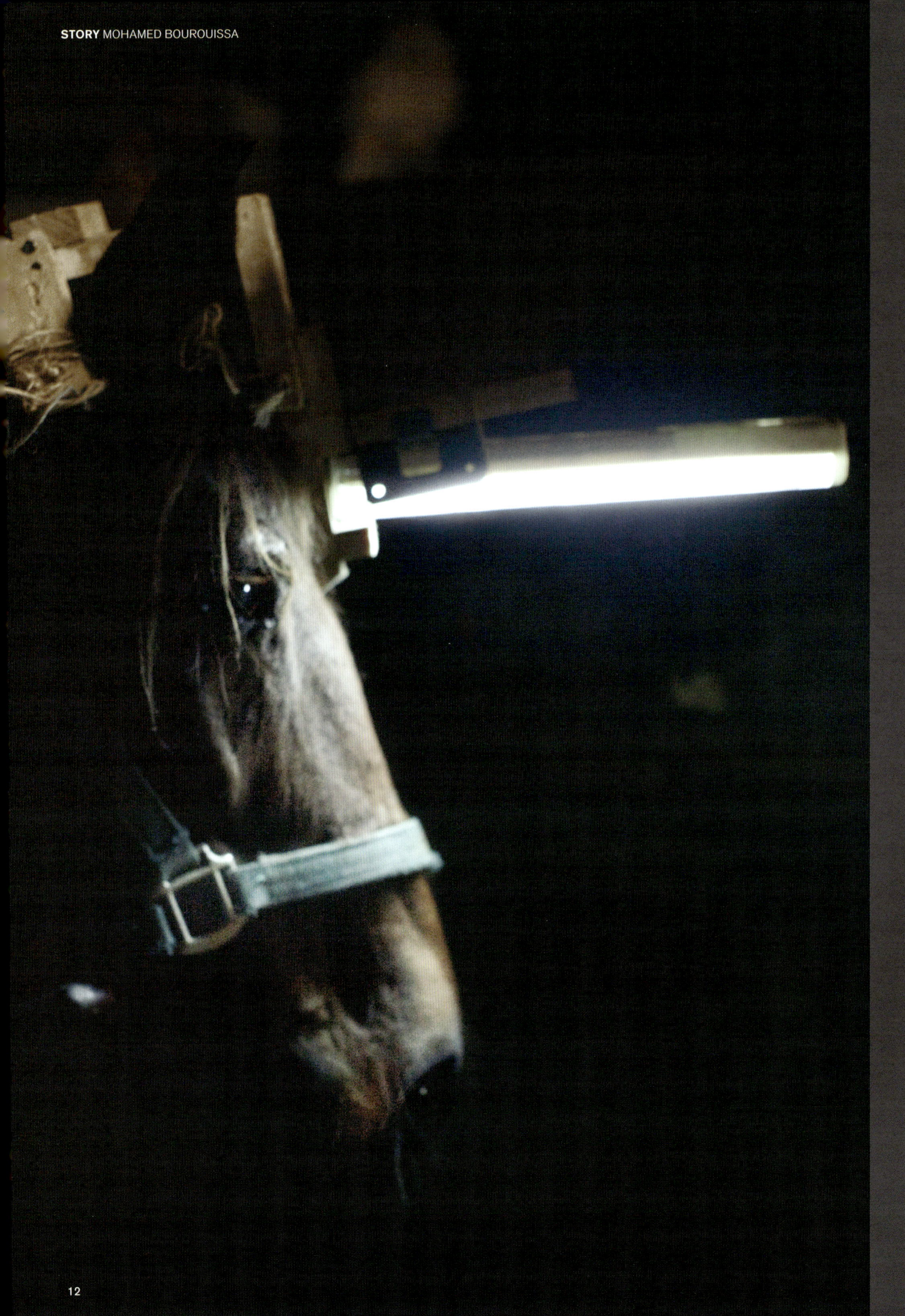

inside his prison cell. The grainy camera phone images were then printed life-size and meticulously installed in the gallery, in as close an approximation to the prison cell layout as possible. Here Bourouissa, along with the viewer, could literally enter a world formed and reconstructed through the eyes of the person inside. While the work emerged through a text message dialogue, in the end it was the person who, by social standards, had been rendered powerless calling the shots.

With these pieces there are the obvious links to the traditions of portraiture and to documentary tropes, but what is becoming increasingly obvious as Bourouissa's practice develops, is the platform for collaboration at its core. Most recently the artist spent time living and working in a north Philadelphia neighborhood, in and around Fletcher Street, on the edge of Fairmount Park. Bourouissa first became interested in the Fletcher Street community through images taken by Brooklyn-based photographer Martha Camarillo. In her photographs he encountered a group of black horsemen—urban cowboys—who had for generations run and maintained stables in Philadelphia. While Camarillo focused on what was described in her publication *Fletcher Street* as the "ghetto" aspect of the Philadelphia subculture, Bourouissa became interested in the optics of a black-inner city community, where the potent symbol of the horse was central. From Bourouissa's perspective as a European looking in, horses had always been synonymous with power and linked historically to the political and social elite. He had grown accustomed to seeing canvases in museums where horses featured prominently alongside strident, conquering Napoleonic figures and the conquistadors. Yet in Fletcher Street and the surrounding area, Bourouissa encountered a landscape in which horses were part of everyday life, albeit in a deconstructed, demythologized urban Western where the archetypal imagery of John Wayne or the silent Marlboro Man had no place.

Rather than simply documenting or fetishizing the romanticism surrounding the horsemen (who are by now accustomed to outsiders coming in to photograph them and taking their leave), and rather than focusing on allusions of poverty or disenfranchisement, Bourouissa began to live and work alongside the Fletcher Street cowboys, wanting to find a way to collaborate and not merely observe. He took on everyday jobs in the stables, cleaning the stalls and shoveling manure. Over time, he developed a relationship to the men that was deeper than the photogenic veneer. What has emerged from this relationship is a new body of works in which the power of the American Western (and all of its symbolism) is literally turned on its head. Instead of John Wayne or a fictional narrative of land and liberty, we are faced with works that include an upside down image of a young man atop a horse embodying what Bourouissa calls "the negative of a cowboy." In his work with the horsemen, the artist has managed to subvert our perceptions of exoticism and the iconography of the past, and instead this new series speaks boldly to the power his collaborators understand they possess.

The resulting film, titled Horse Day, *and a new photographic series were unveiled this fall as part of* Capsule 02: Mohamed Bourouissa *at Haus der Kunst in Munich.*

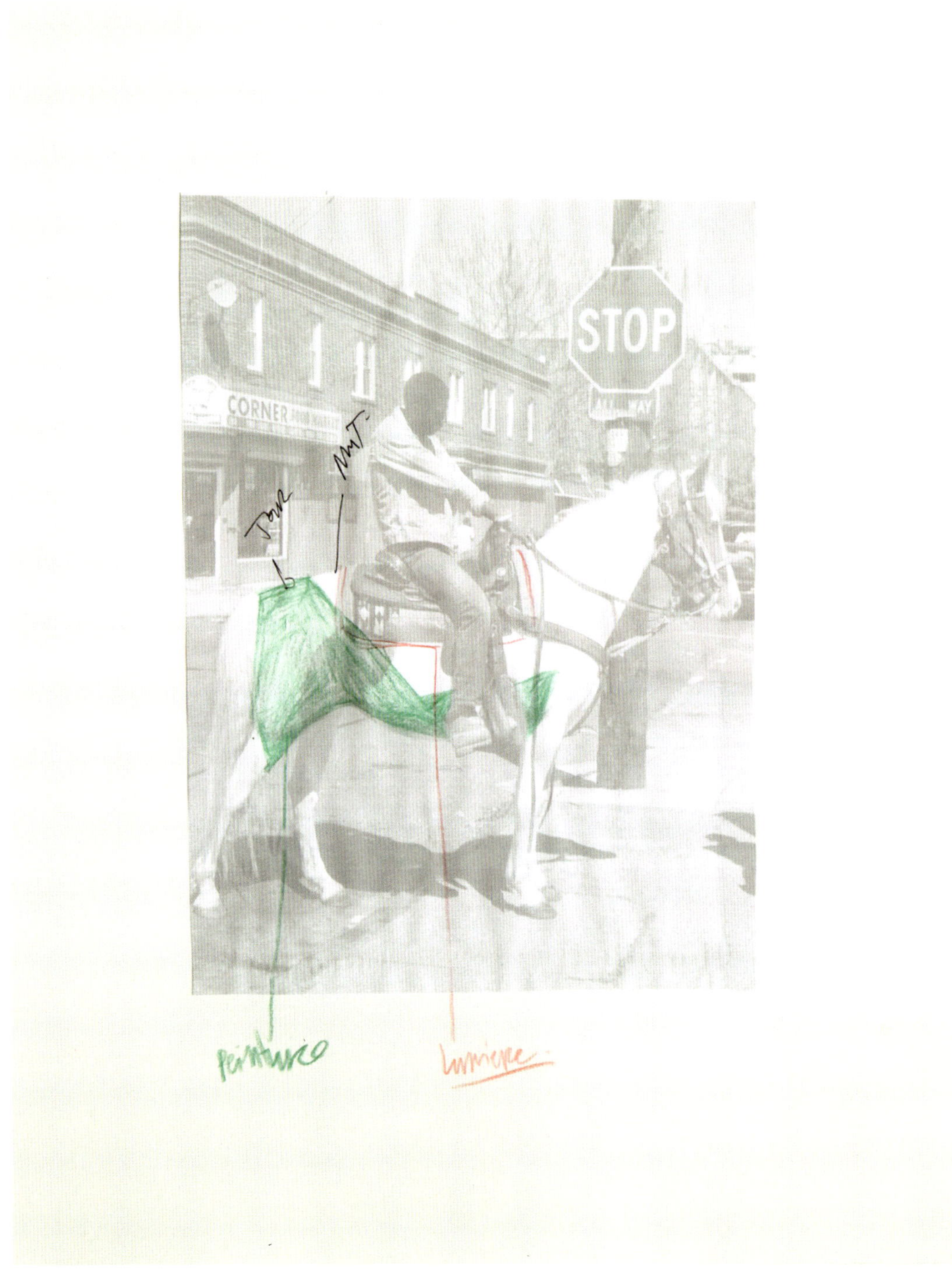

Sans Titre (2014)

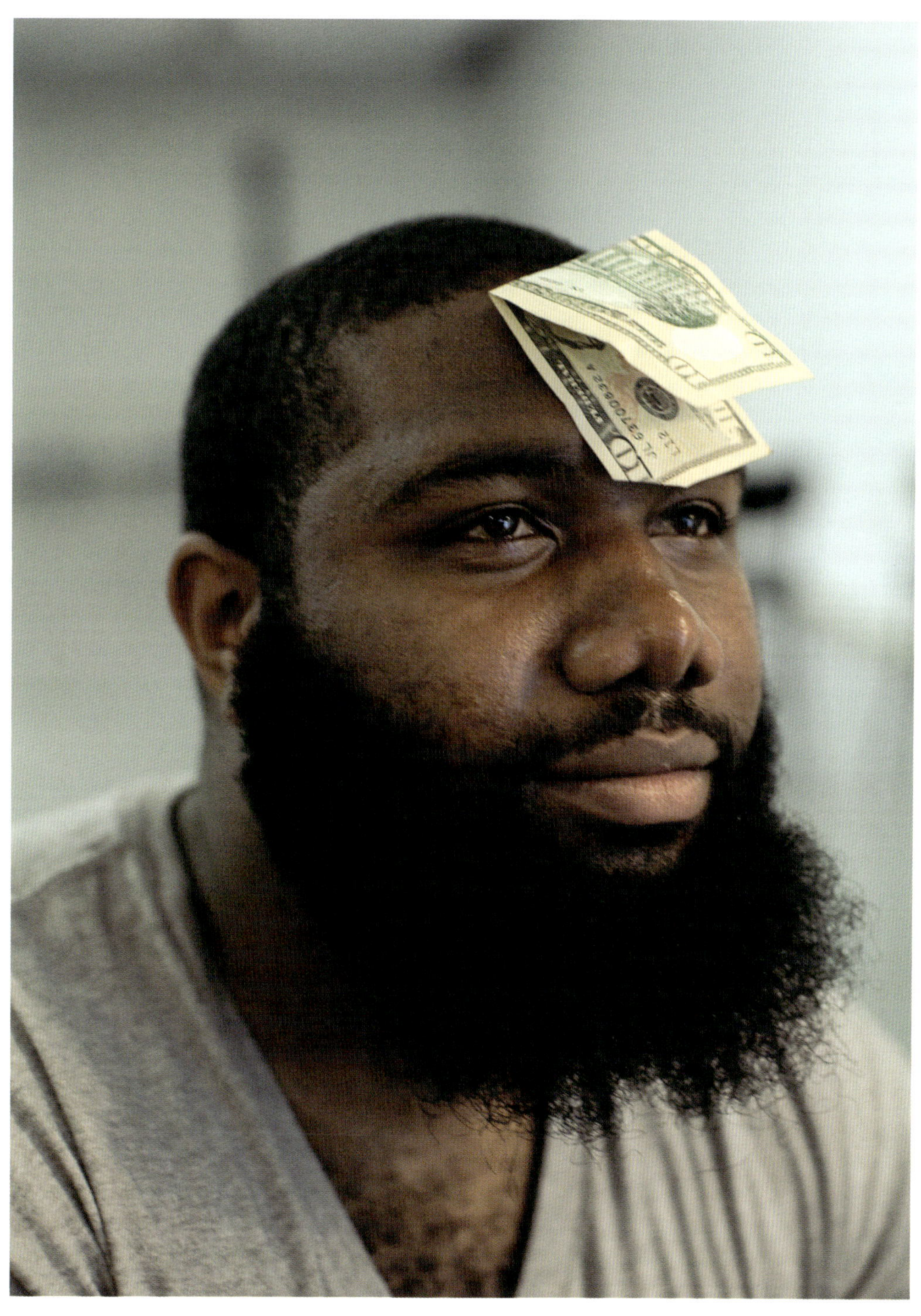

Skin and paper (2014)

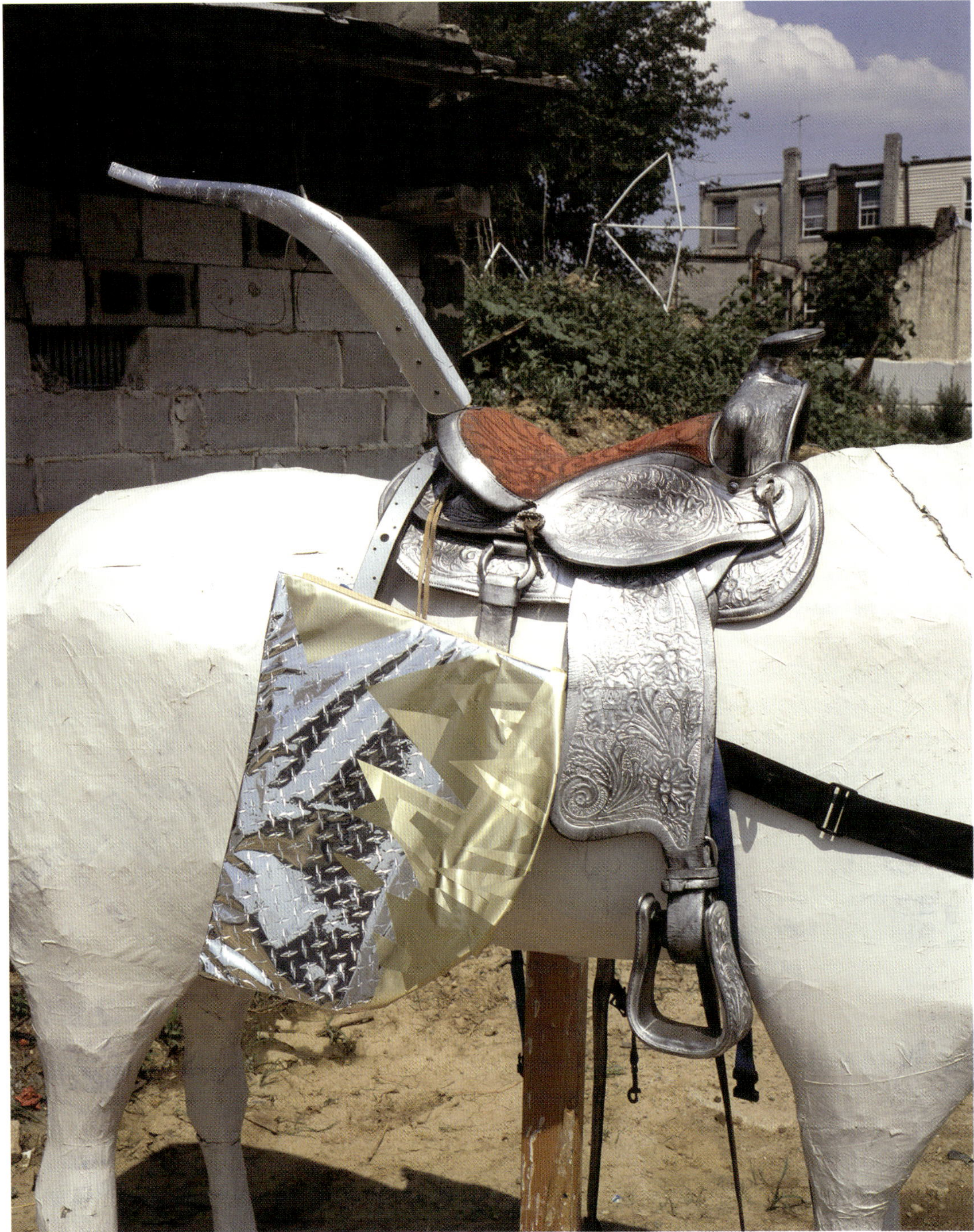

Pegasus (2014)

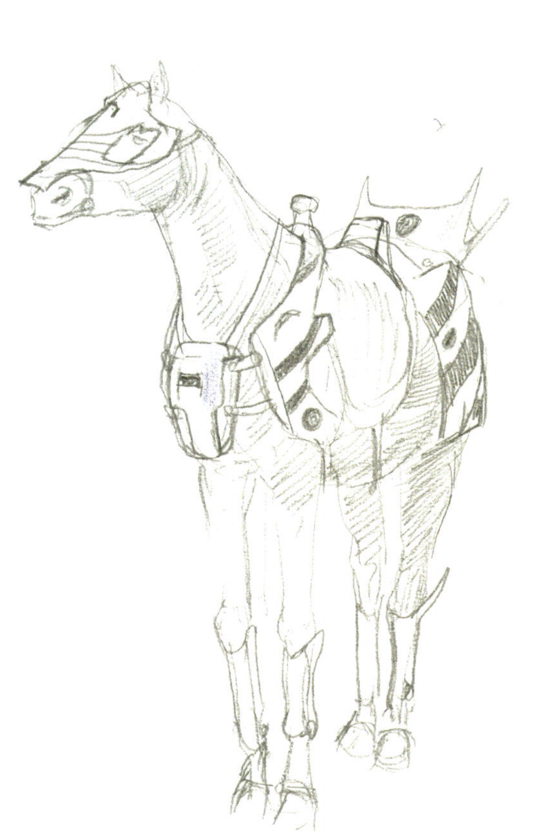

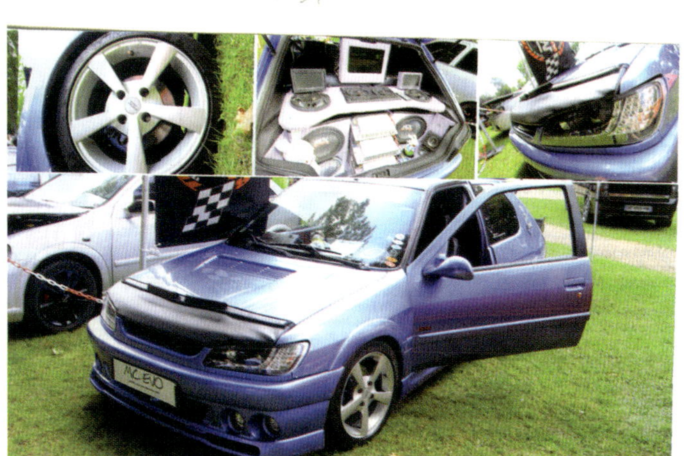

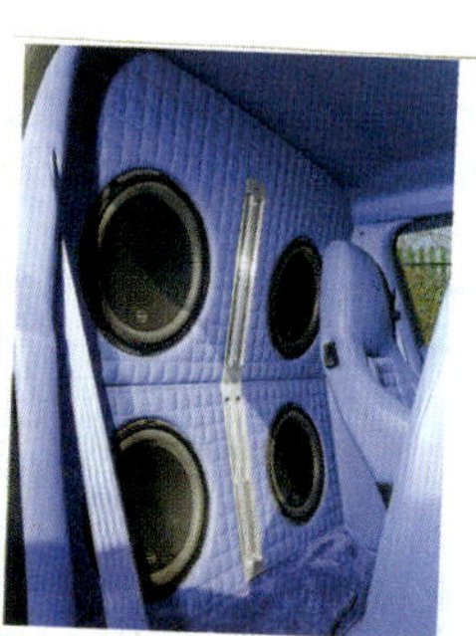

Exit la banquette arrière, Andrew a choisi le son à ses invités. C'est son choix !

Sans Titre (2014)

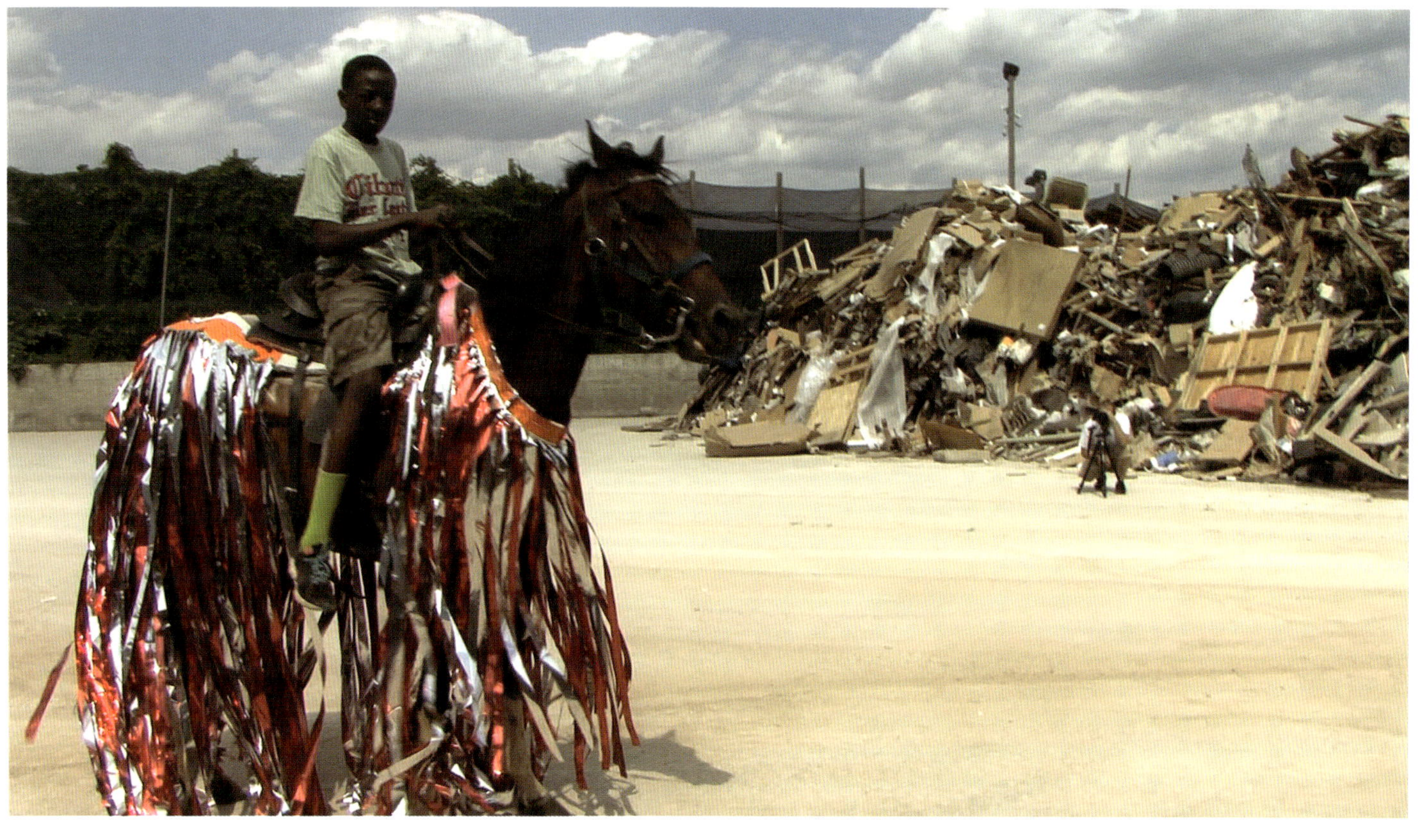

Film still, *Horse Day* (2014)

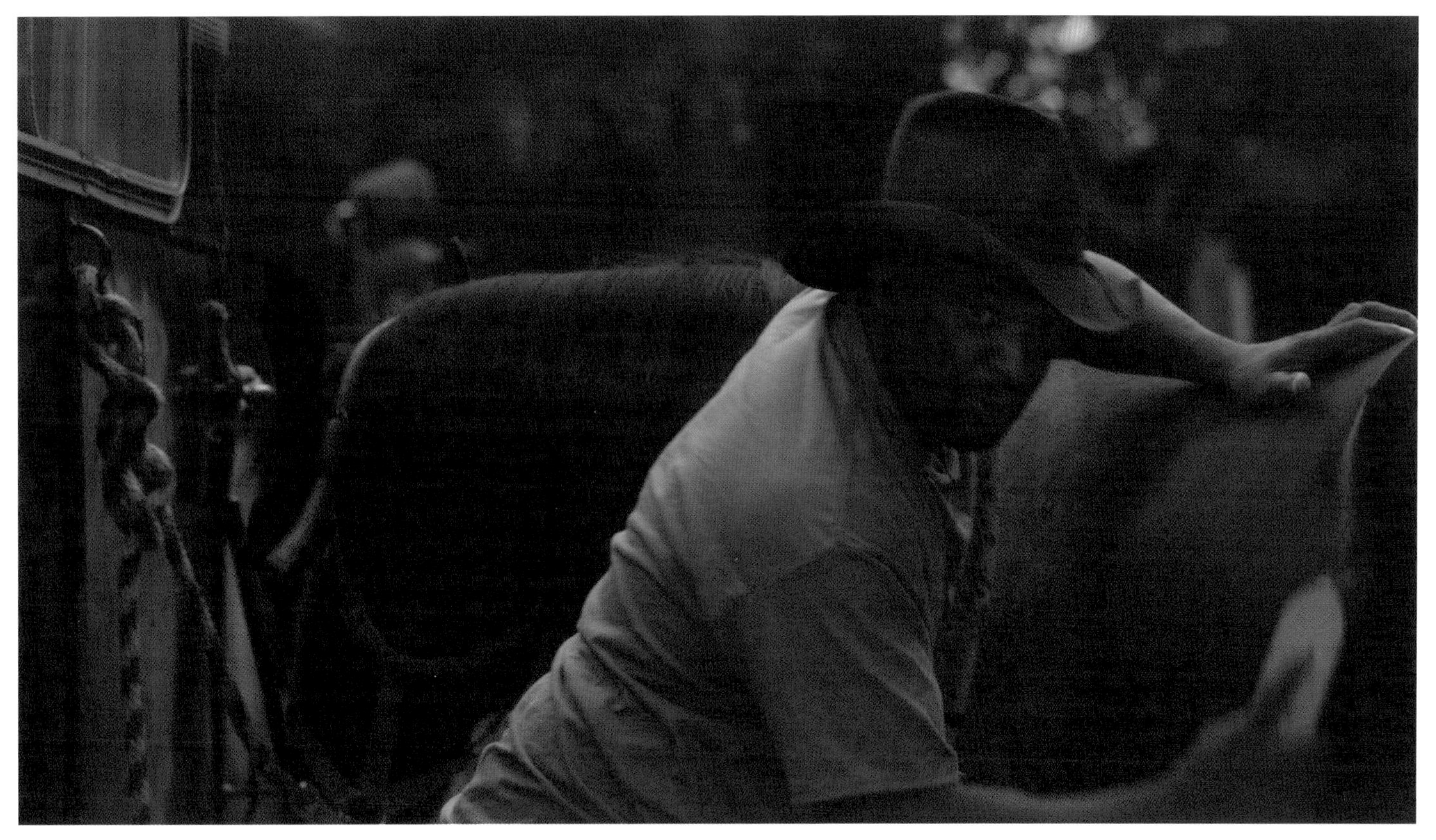

Film still, *Horse Day* (2014)

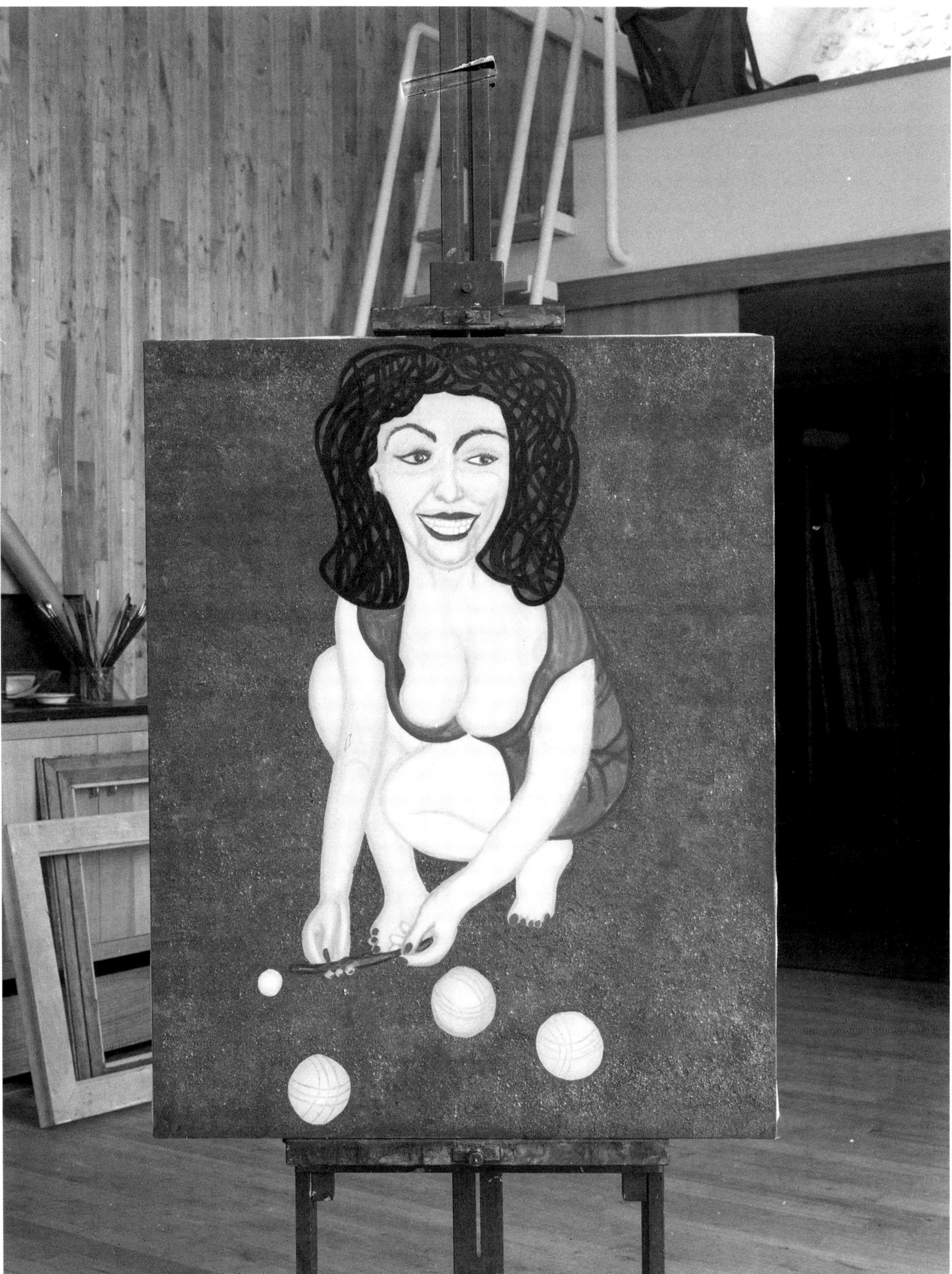

Iris Jouante (1961)

William Copley

INTRODUCED BY HIS GALLERIST **NICHOLAS OLNEY**

In March 1951, William N. Copley, along with his girlfriend Gloria de Herrara and the newly married Man and Juliette Ray, boarded the *S.S. DeGrasse* bound from New York to Paris. Marcel and Teeny Duchamp saw them off at the port, Marcel handing Man his model for *Female Fig Leaf* to be cast in bronze by a foundry in Paris. Copley, having closed his short-lived but seminal Surrealist gallery in Beverly Hills in 1949, had embarked on his dream to become an expatriate artist in Paris. For the next twelve years Copley devoted himself to painting and creative activity, leaving behind what he referred to as the intellectual wasteland of Los Angeles.

Bill married Noma Ratner on December 31, 1953 (Man was best man and Julie was maid of honor) and purchased a home in Longpont-Sur-Orge outside of Paris near Orly airport. The town is now absorbed into the outskirts of the city, but in the 1950s it was very much considered the country, though close enough that one could pop into town for dinner without trouble. There he engaged his friends, the British Modernist architects Jane Drew and Maxwell Frye, to design a small but beautiful new studio in an outbuilding in the garden—built with local stone over an existing root cellar—with a sweeping curved roof, loft, and skylight. Bill and Noma entertained often, but Copley was dedicated to his work in the studio, typically painting nine to five, six days a week.

Before the new studio was completed, Bill worked in a smaller space across a courtyard from the house. During this time he would have taken finished paintings outside or into the house to be photographed. Noma, who was a meticulous record keeper, would have wanted photos of every completed work. Inside the house, it would have been dry and there was enough room to set up the camera. The couple's furnishings, Bill's collection, and objects from everyday life populated in the background.

Working with the Copley estate to digitize their archives and lay the groundwork for an eventual catalogue raisonné, we came across a batch of 4 x 5-inch negatives of Bill's paintings, photographed in his house and studio. This was a great find, as it contained crucial visual records of paintings that Copley had made while living in Longpont. Once scanned and brought up on screen as positive images, we immediately saw that these pictures serve as a captivating account not just of individual canvases but a visual record of the house and studio and their contents. Like a time capsule, each image becomes a window into a lost moment in time.

In the Copley archives there are versions of these images that were cropped to the edge of the canvas to be used for catalogues, advertisements, and to maintain an archive of his works. These images would also have been sent to collectors as a sales tool. Copley was an easel painter, and to photograph his paintings he didn't hang them on the wall, but propped the up with what he had at hand. It's difficult to ascertain why these photographs were taken the way they were with so much additional information in the background. Jacqueline Hyde, the presumed photographer, was a student of Man Ray, and she may have been experimenting with her own ideas and technique or working at Bill's instruction.

There's the picture itself—the completed painting that is ostensibly the subject—perfectly exposed and ready to be cropped for reproduction. But because the tripod has been deliberately set back from the paintings a broader story is revealed. In the margins we can see parts of works in Copley's collection by Wilfredo Lam, Joseph Cornell, Max Ernst, Man Ray, and Francis Picabia. We see the Mexican folk objects that Bill kept in his studio, and on shelves and in stacks, his collection of books ranging from a MAD magazine compendium to surveys of pre-Colombian and Cycladic Art. It's a keyhole view into the types of things Bill was looking at and excited by, at a critical moment when he was forging his myriad interests into his own unique voice.

What are Copley's possible influences here? Certainly Man Ray was one, and in fact there exists a great archive of Man Ray photographs taken in the house as well. Prior to meeting Noma and moving to Longpont, Bill's Paris studio was next to Brancusi's on the impasse Ronsin, and quite likely the young artist would have been taken by Brancusi's own stunning photographs of sculptures in his studio. While surely artworks in their own right, these photographs were also effectively used (and indeed by Brancusi's dealer and friend Duchamp) to show collectors in America what was new and for sale in the studio.

There is something else going on in Bill's photographs: the arrangements of backgrounds and the selection of where to shoot implies intent. Was there a particular purpose, or was Bill's life in Paris so aesthetically driven from morning to night that he couldn't help but make each action as visually interesting as possible? The desire to have them be more than just a photograph of a painting seems evident. Much like Copley's paintings themselves, the compositions of the photographs have a casual quality that fails to obscure their underlying sophistication.

To me this illuminates one of the great dichotomies in the man— that Bill was simultaneously a primitive and a sophisticate. The ongoing dialogue between these poles is part of what makes him so fascinating. It's a joy to look back in time and feel his excitement at the opportunity to throw himself headlong into painting, supported by a community of friends and heroes. With the gift of this wideangle perspective, which allows the edges of the world into the frame, the paintings become even more alive.

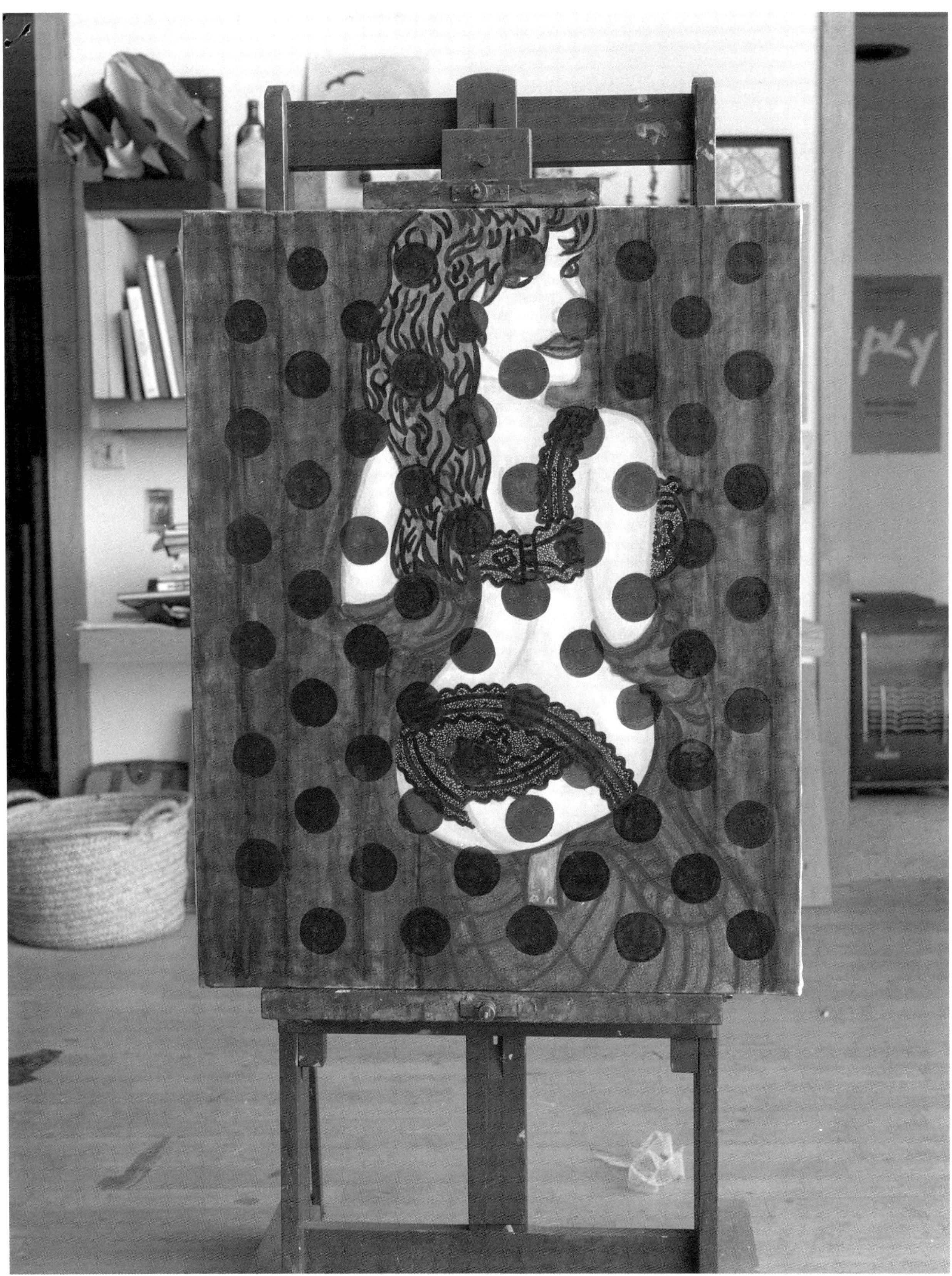

Lily Niagra No. 2 (1962)

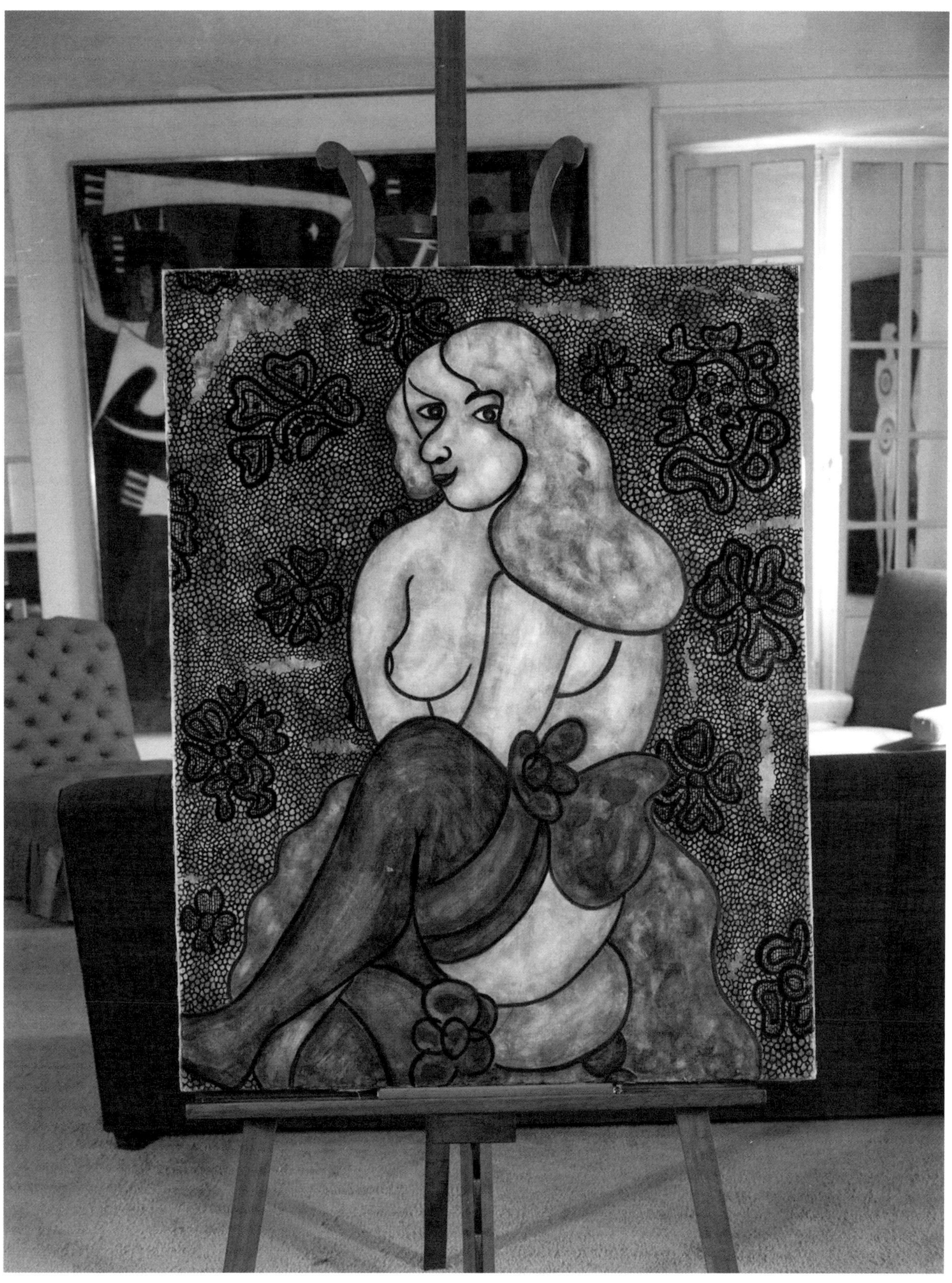

Persephone (1960)

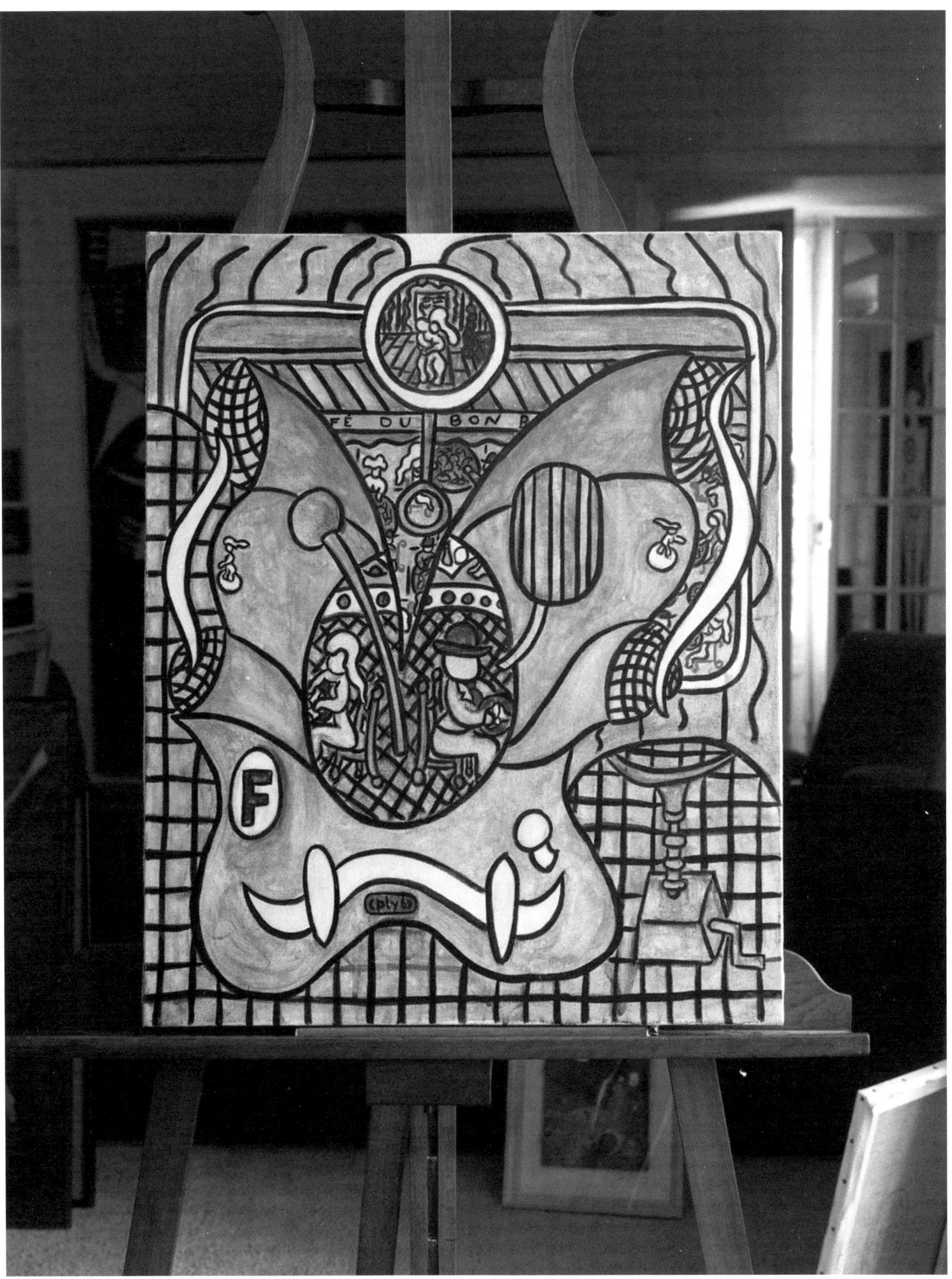

Cafe du Bon B (1960)

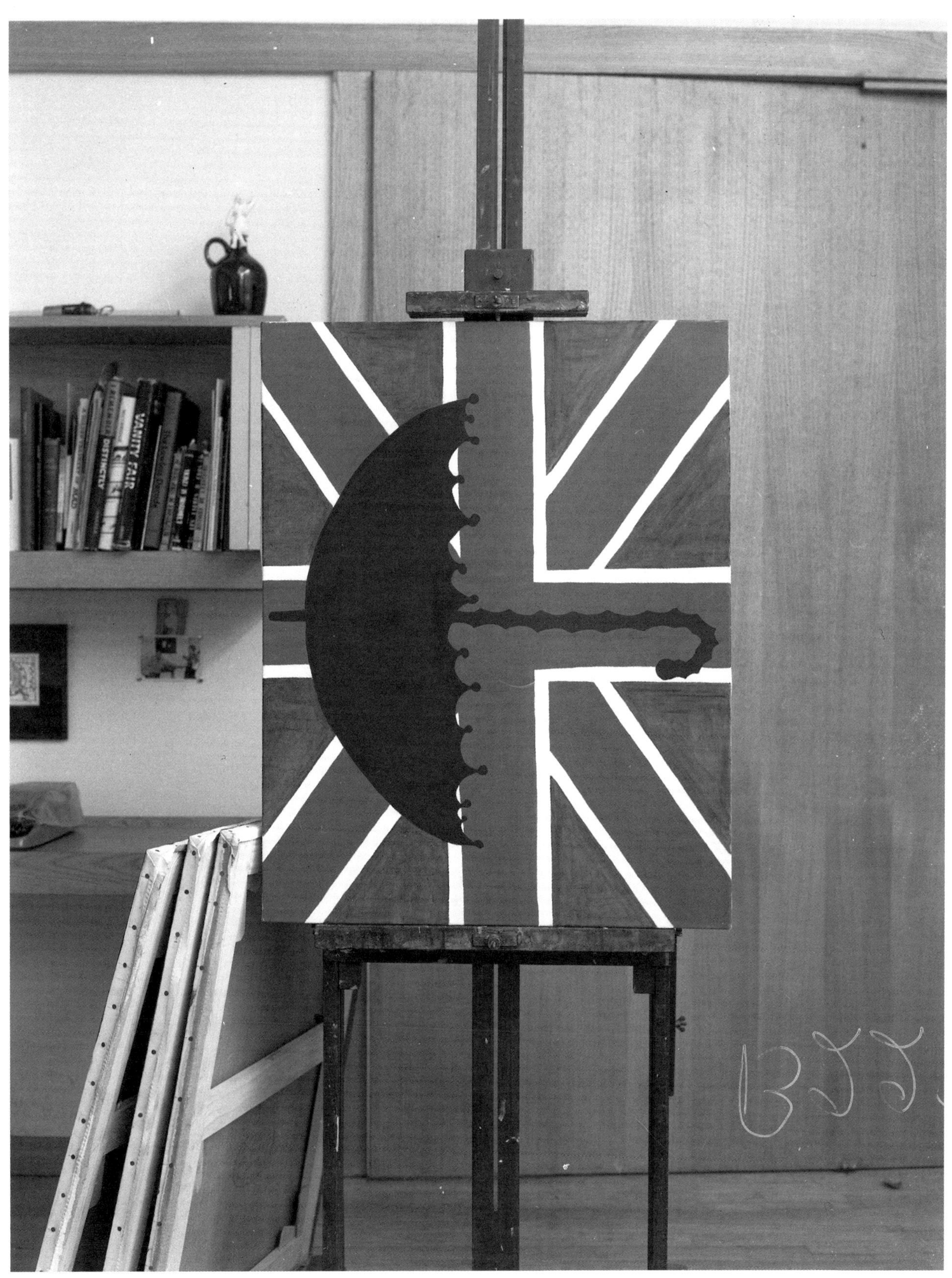

Model for English Flag (1961)

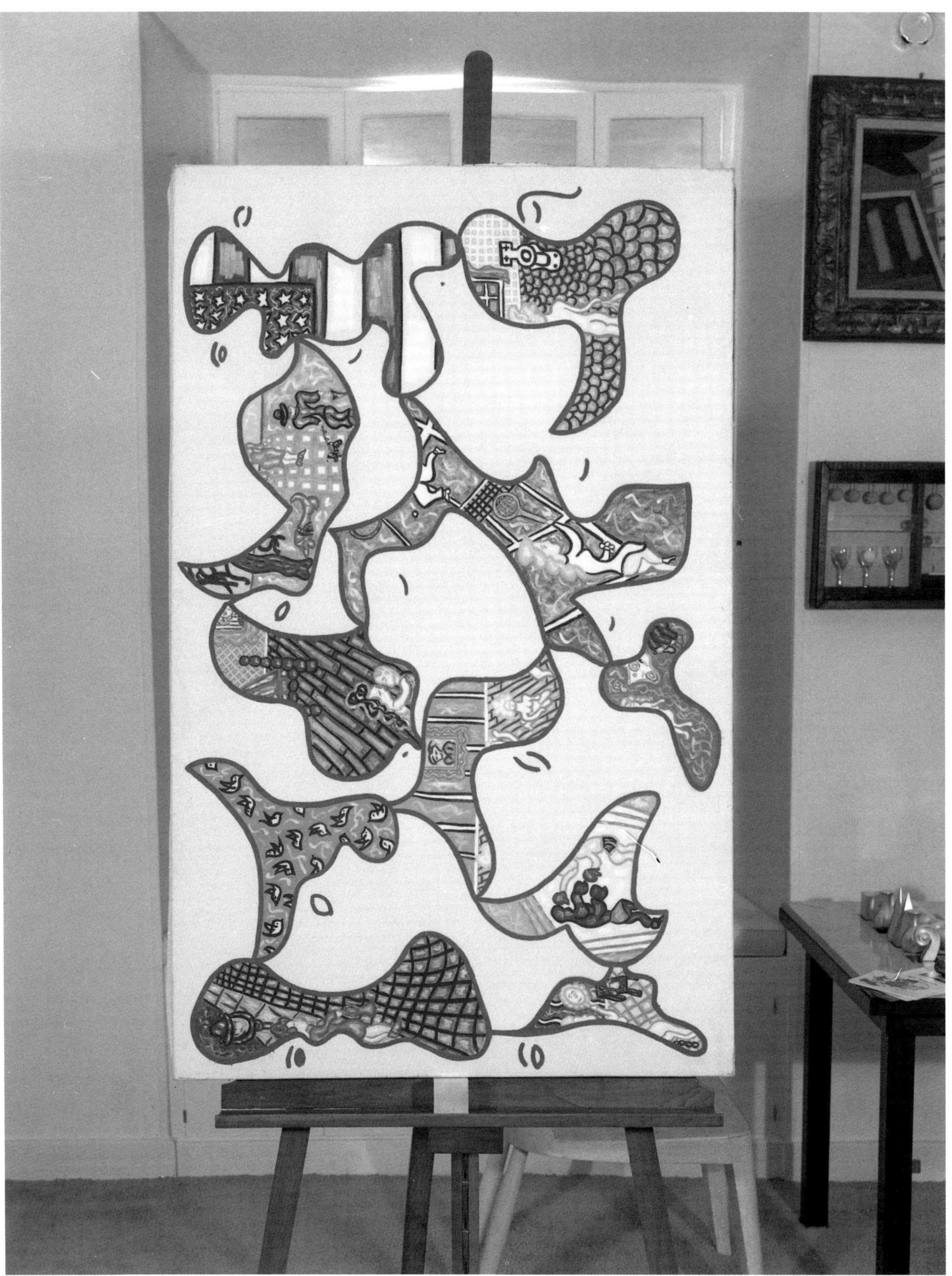

Jigsaw Puzzle (1957)

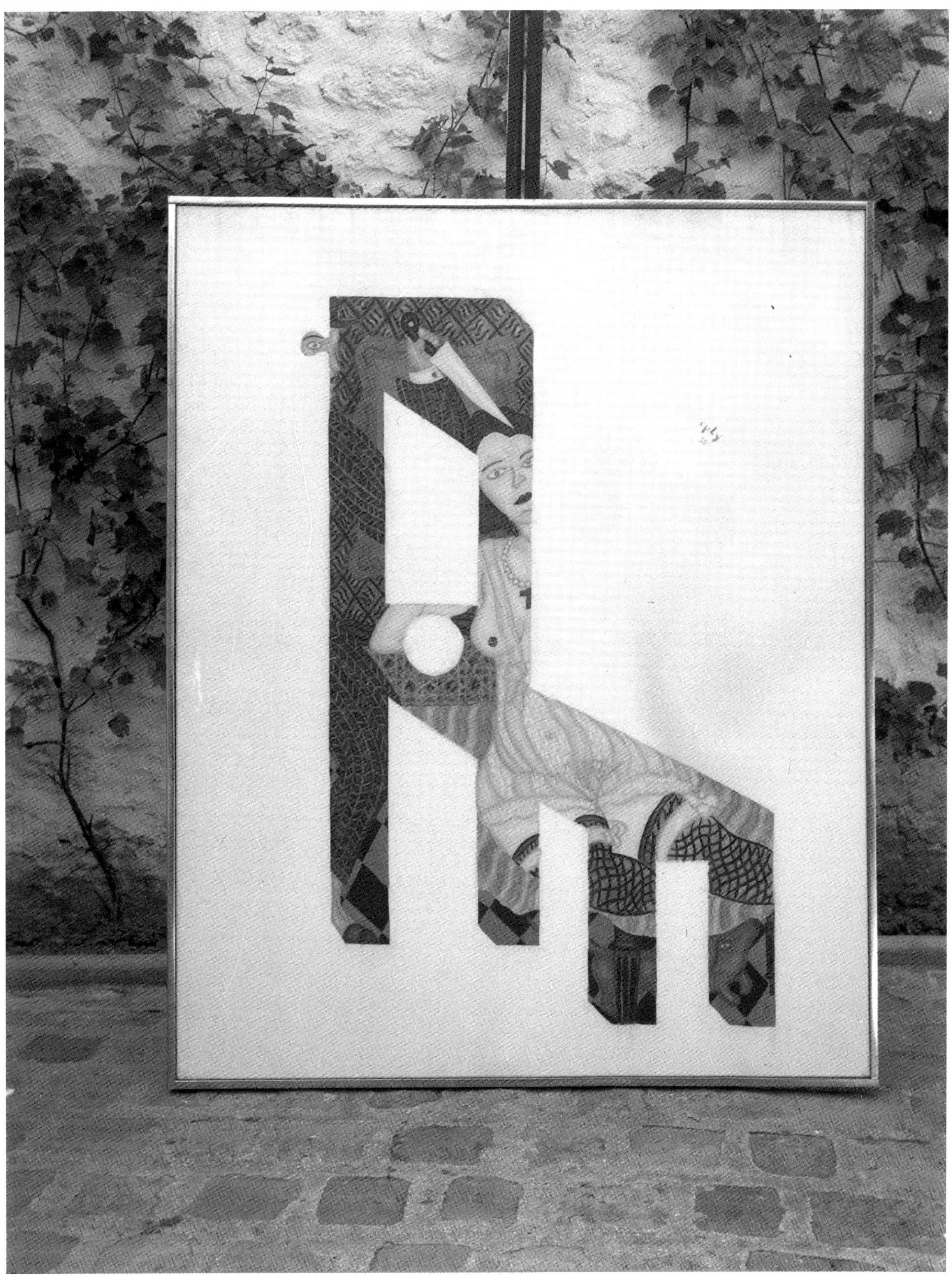

Pharmacie (1958)

FROM KING TO CAMUS...

ISOLDE BRIELMAIER MEETS **WARDELL MILAN**

Wardell Milan (born 1978) earned a BFA in photography and painting in 2001 at the University of Tennessee, in his home town of Knoxville. He then went on to earn an MFA at Yale University in 2004. Right out of school in 2005, Milan emerged and was included in institutional exhibitions such as *Greater New York* at PS1 Contemporary Art Center and *Frequency* at The Studio Museum in Harlem, and had his first solo gallery show at Taxter and Spengermann Gallery. Milan has continued to challenge conventions of medium and message in his deeply personal and prolific work. For this issue of *OSMOS Magazine,* Wardell Milan converses with curator and friend Isolde Brielmaier.

ISOLDE BRIELMAIER You move back and forth between—and within—different mediums. Can you talk about where you started and where you are now in terms of combining your photography, painting, and drawings?

WARDELL MILAN From an early age, I've had an interest in making work in a number of different mediums. As adolescent I began drawing, and for a number of years the pencil and charcoal were my medium of choice. For my ninth or tenth birthday, my uncle gave me a 35mm Pentex camera. Soon after being gifted the camera, photography became an important medium in the development of my creativity. It wasn't until my undergraduate studies, and a number of painting classes, that the medium of painting became a true inter-

est of mine. During this time I slowly began to understand how to work with all three mediums in a more integrated way.

IB What about the relationship between your many bodies of work? For example, there is a focus on the body and on physicality and movement in many of your images. Do you see this and other elements as threads linking your work over the years?

WM Absolutely, the themes of physicality and movement; of sexuality and morality, my personal history and obsessions, as well as larger histories—many of these themes and conversations are threaded through the different bodies of work. The themes aren't always interpreted or visualized with the same artistic expression from one body of work to the next, but the conceptual and narrative conversations I'm interested in having with the work move from one series of works to the next.

IB I know that you create elaborate and intricate dioramas that you then photograph. Your process is quite labor intensive and multilayered, though you have never shown the dioramas (and you often destroy them or store them away). Can you share a bit about this process?

WM It has taken a long time to get this point with the construction of the dioramas. The development of these three-dimensional constructions began during my graduate studies at Yale. Over the years the construction of the dioramas has become more and more sophisticated. There's a strong understanding of how important it is to build

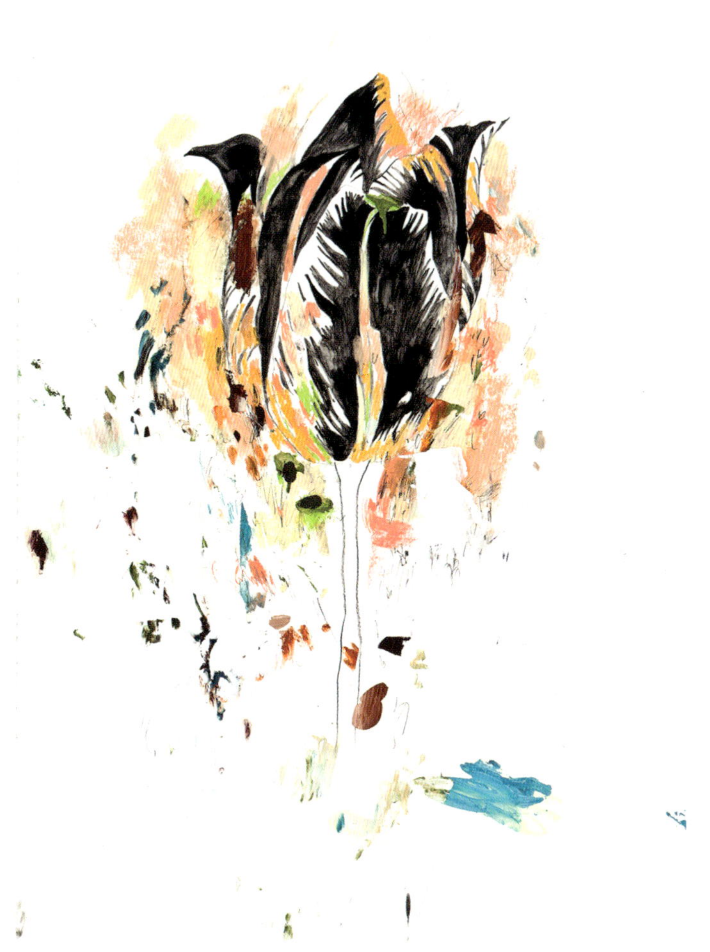 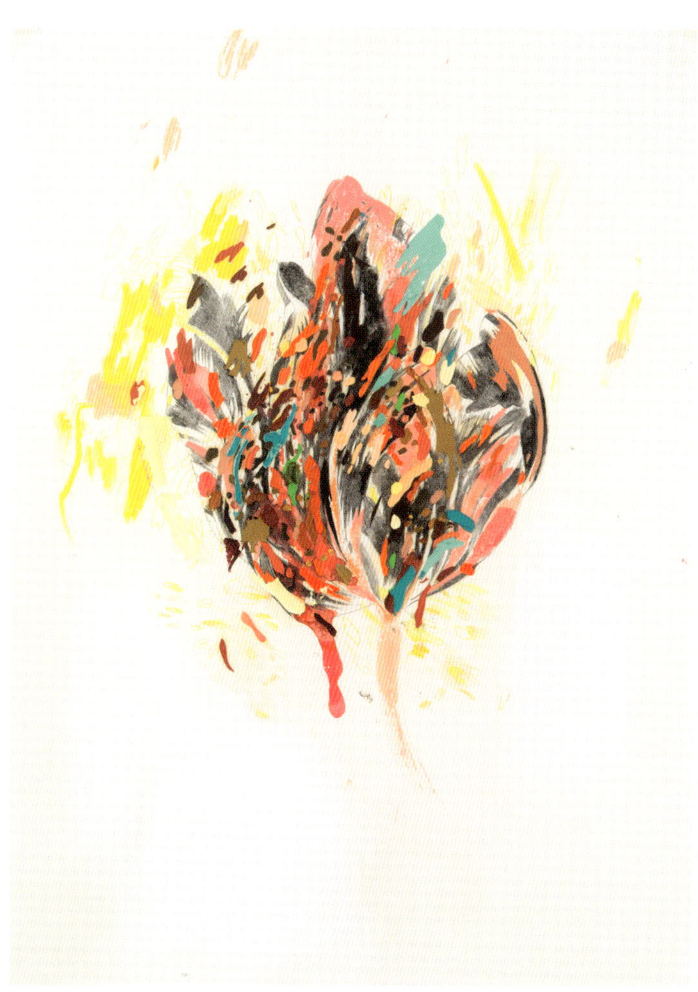

these worlds with the aid of the camera, having it positioned in front on the developing diorama, and consistently looking through camera lens as I build a landscape or an interior to insure that an interesting composition is developing. That information that shouldn't be seen, isn't in view in of the lens. And most importantly, my oscillation between the camera and the diorama helps with the creation of an optical illusion. I'm also thinking about the final presentation of the diorama, which is a photograph. The photograph is how the audience will experience these constructions. When building a diorama, I'm always considering the viewer's potential visual experience. Years ago I would start a diorama with little preparation. Perhaps I'd make a quick sketch of what I wanted to build with a partially resolved conceptual idea. I now find that mode of working to be counterproductive. With the dioramas I now build, I spend a lot of time sketching out the form or layout of the diorama. Conceptually and thematically, I have a clear understanding as to what the narrative(s) of the scene will be. And all the while I invest a ton of time searching for pictures and images to appropriate and use in the dioramas.

IB Your art is often grounded in extended research. How do you go about this process? Do you begin with an idea or does your reading enable you to develop your concepts?

WM The development of the work comes from my own personal curiosities and interest as well as from the many different essays, articles, and books I read. Most often what I'm reading is a text I've

searched for with the hope that it will further educate or better inform an idea or topic I've been considering. Literature has been a huge influence on my work and creative practice. Presently, it is the work of Albert Camus and Eugene Ionesco that has my interest. Although, I do plan on starting to read Steven King's book *IT* about a scary murderous clown that lives underneath a city's streets … . Sometimes one needs a bit of light text after reading *The Myth of Sisyphus*.

IB Your latest series engages ideas, history, and narratives. What source material inspired this new work? What can you tell us about these forthcoming photographs?

WM Three significant readings contributed to the development of my latest series entitled *The Kingdom or Exile* (2013–ongoing): Eugene Ionesco's play *Rhinoceros*, the short stories of Albert Camus, and Charles Baudelaire's most famous work, *Les Fleurs du Mal*. The forthcoming photographs are at times challenging—both visually and in content. The series is actually made up of four different, but related, thematic chapters, the first being *Parisian Landscapes* (2013–2014). The significant themes in this chapter include, the unconscious, voyeurism/exhibitionism, femininity, the supremacy of nature, sexual aberration, and love. Subsequently, the narratives of the photos in this series will relate to these topics.

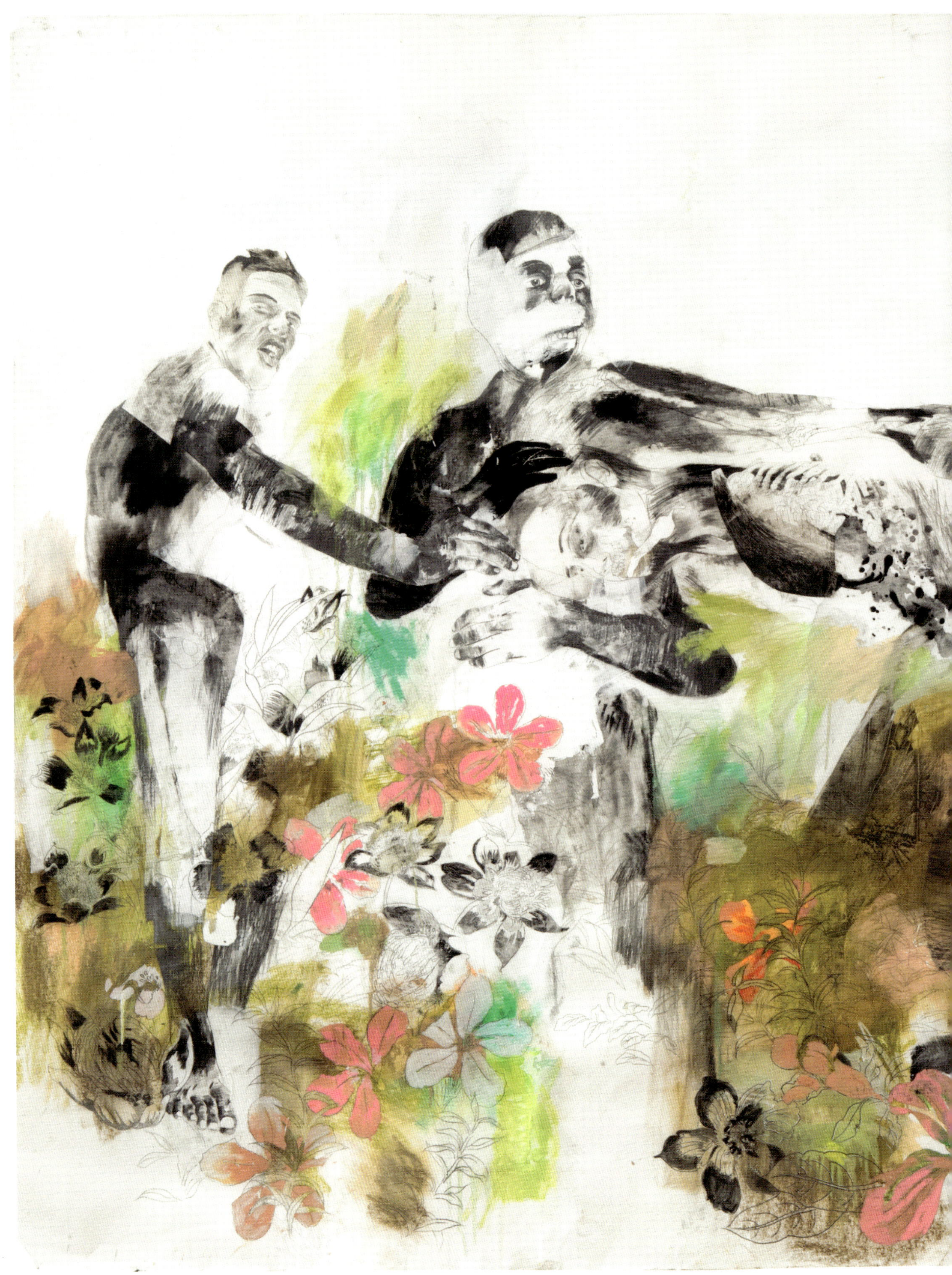

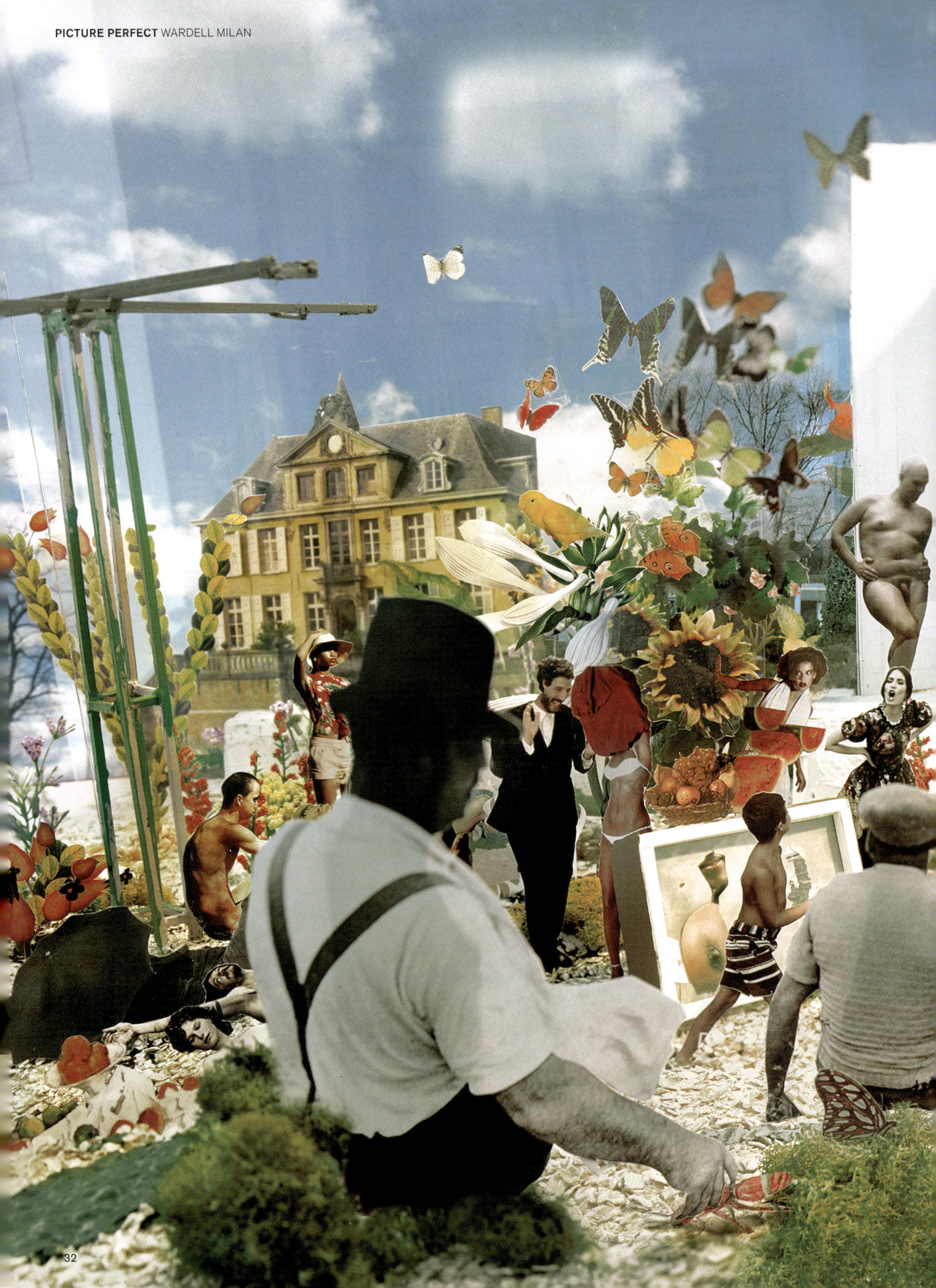

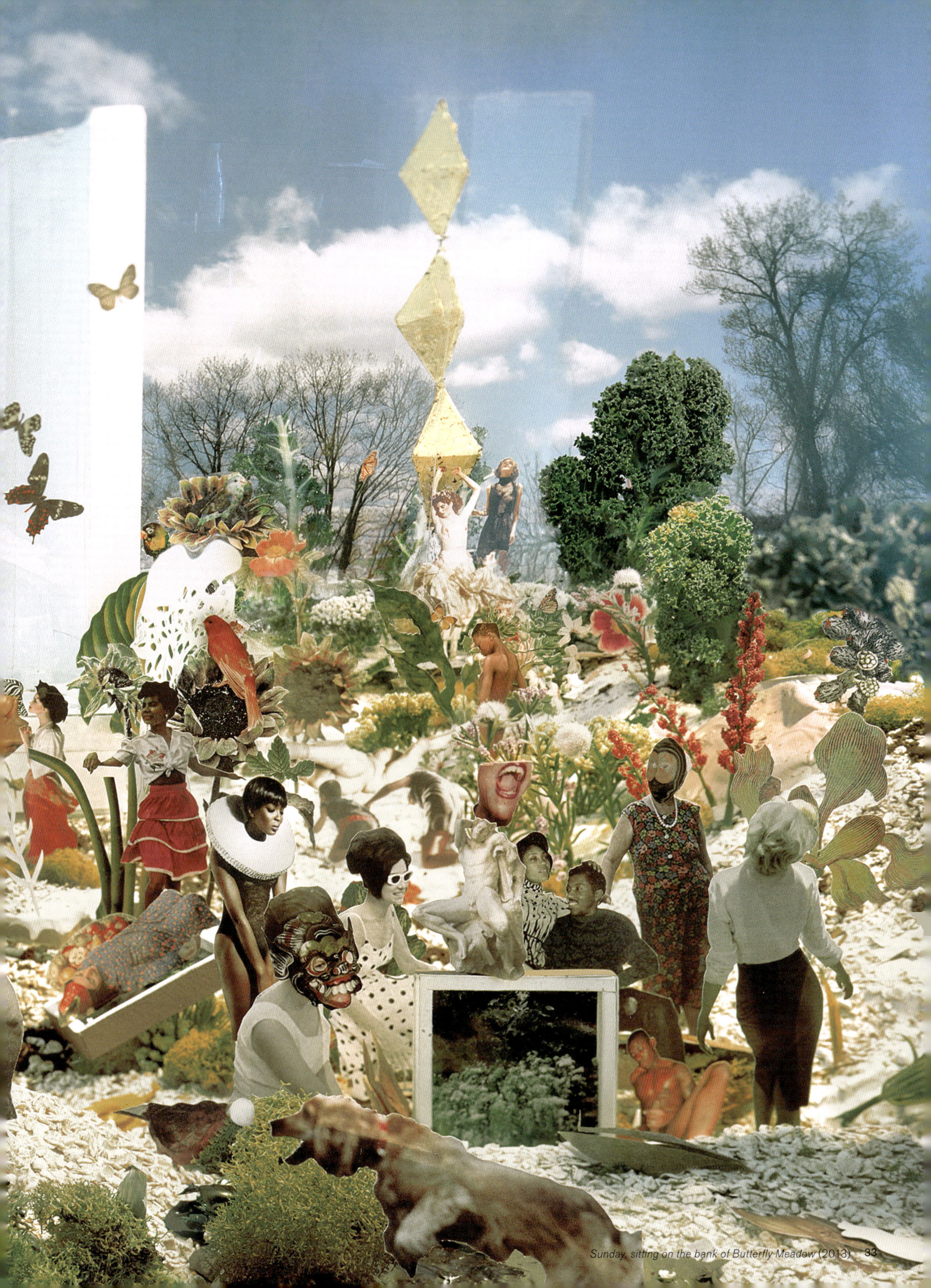

Sunday, sitting on the bank of Butterfly Meadow (2013) 33

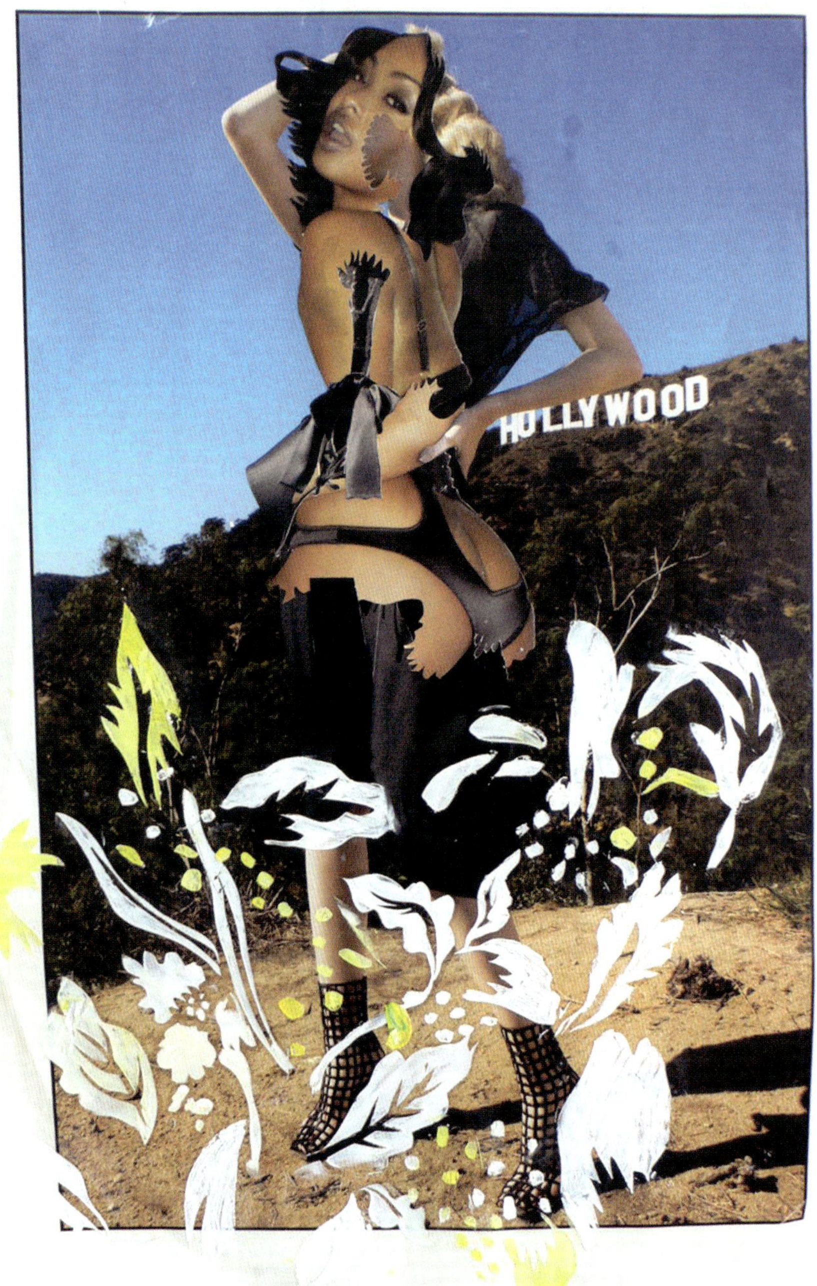

Exotic Perfume (vivica) (2013)

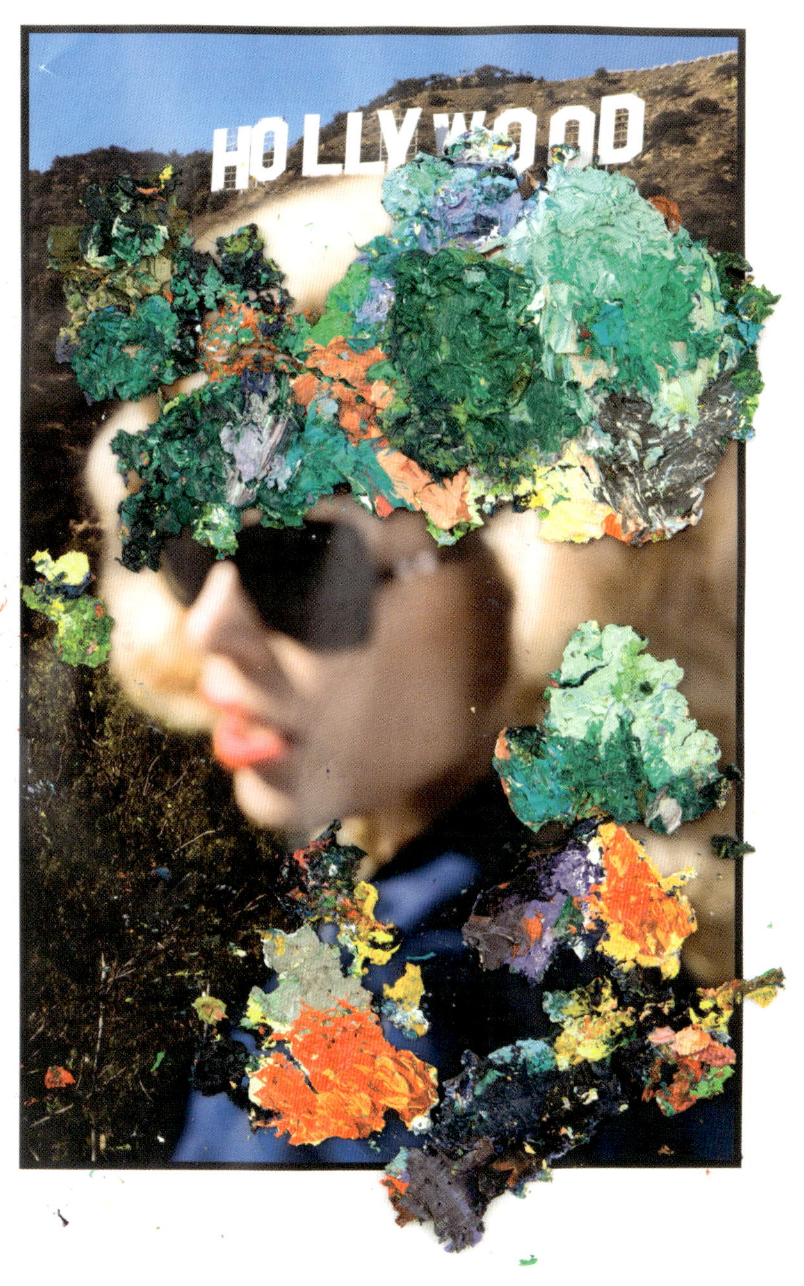

Exotic Perfume (vivica) (2013)

TAMARA RAFKIN
SLEEPING HOUSES
WATCHFUL HOUSES

Safety, security, and personal control are subjects at the core of Tamara Rafkin's photographic practice, whether immediately apparent or in veiled narrative. After relocating to the Flemish part of Belgium in 2005, Rafkin began to notice regional eccentricities that led to the series *Sleeping Houses.*

The residents of Flanders share a cultural habit of shuttering their houses every evening, whether it is warm, cold, light, or dark—what matters is closing out the outside world. Manicured gardens and well-tended houses are shut tight for the night with no signs of interior life, as if standing in wait for someone to awaken them. Towns and villages feel empty, abandoned, surreal to the non-native visitor or resident.

As one travels from Flanders toward the Netherlands at night, no map is necessary to know when you have crossed the border. The Flemish shuttered houses give way to the open and glowing houses of the Dutch countryside; houses whose windows act as beacons on the street, presenting all their contents and actions for the passer-by to see. *The Watchful Houses* of the Netherlands stand awake, waiting to lure you in or bring out the voyeur in you, while presenting an acute awareness of their individual cultural identity.

Tamara Rafkin is an American artist originally from New York living and working in Flanders. Primarily a photographer, Rafkin uses color as an emotive tool between her work and her audience. She continues to work with the chemical processes of film and paper as it affords her the ability to connect in the darkroom with her images in a way that she feels is lost via the computer.

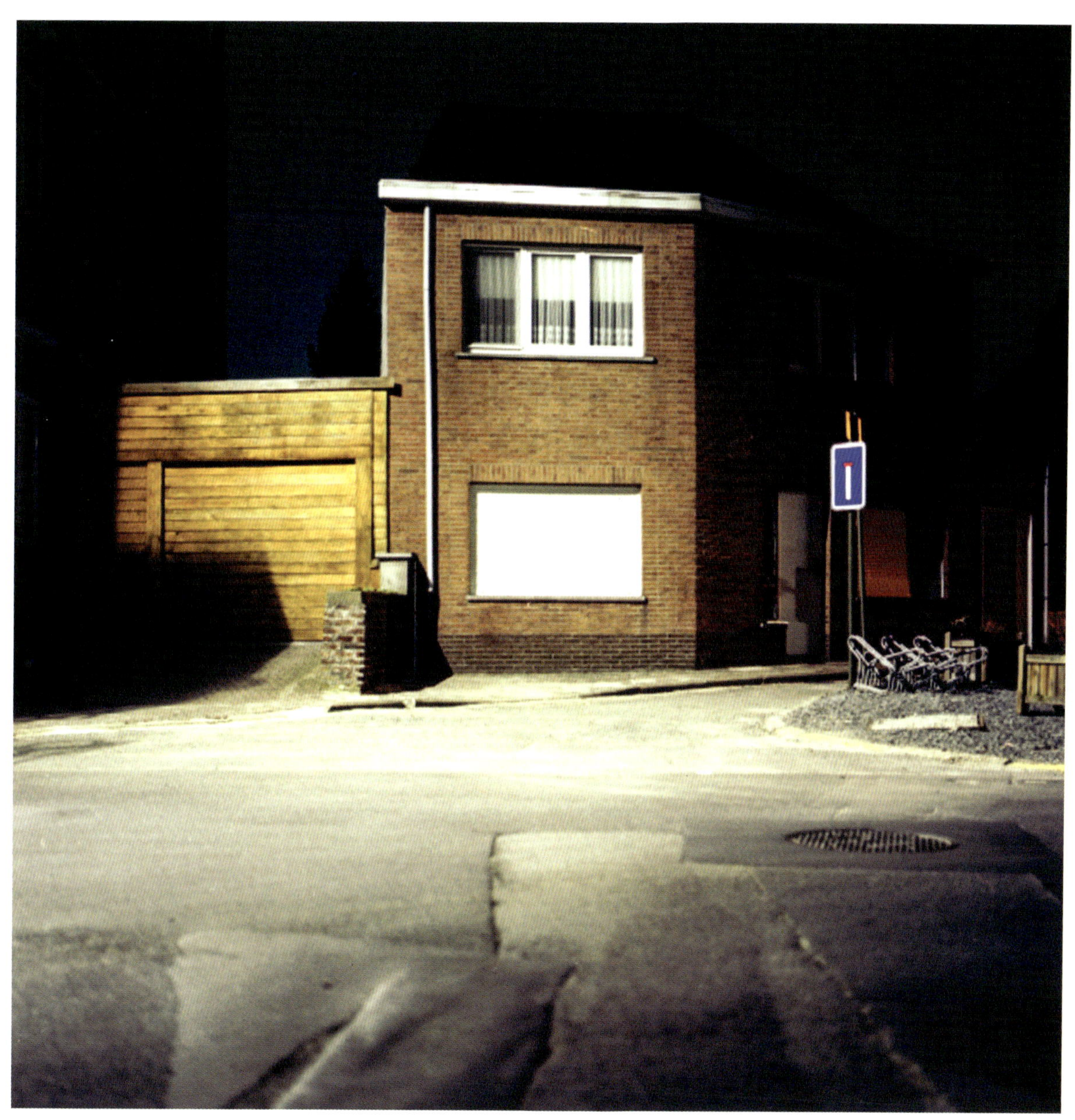

Sleeping Houses 6 (2007)

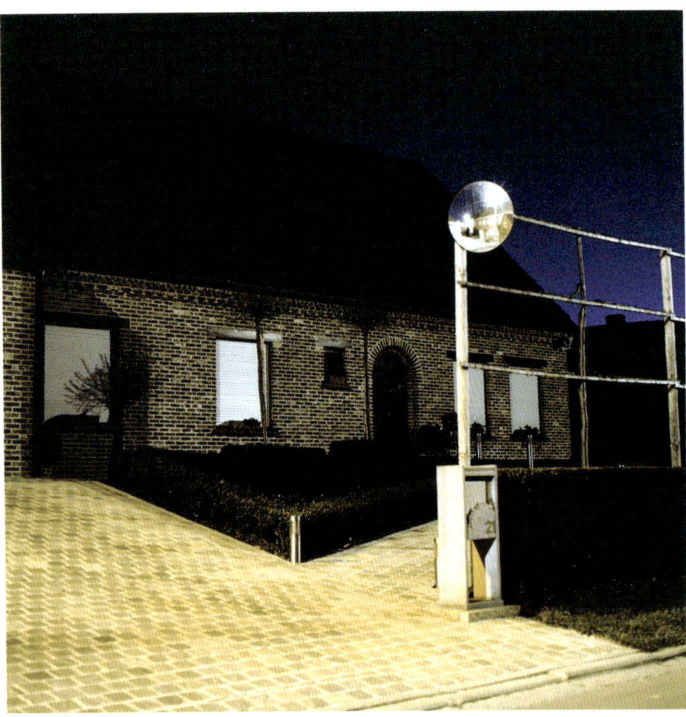

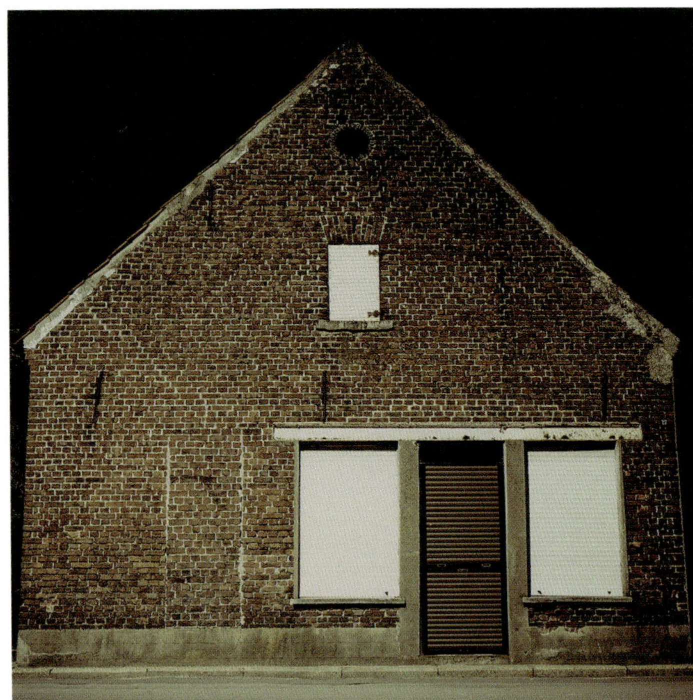

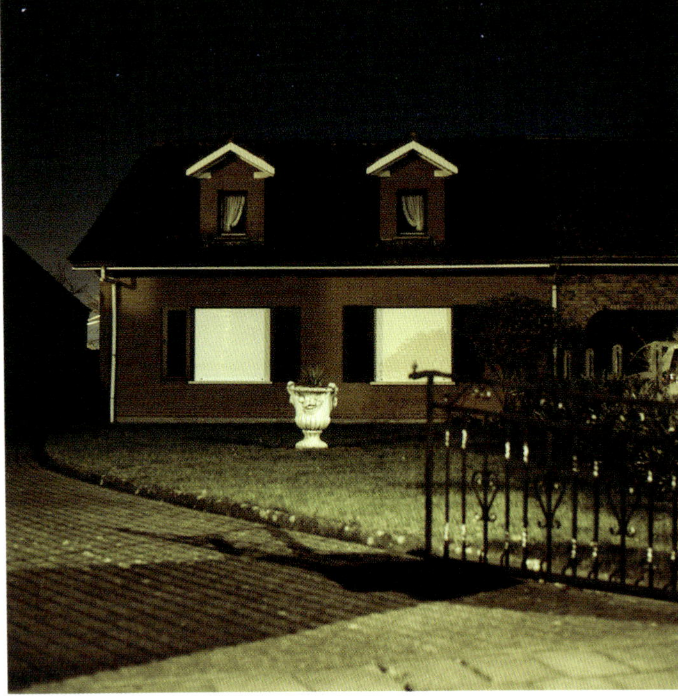

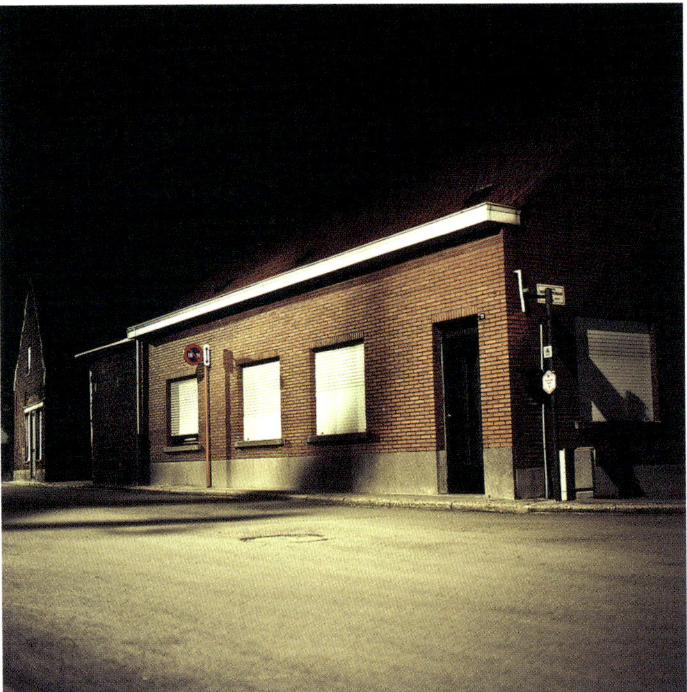

CLOCKWISE FROM TOP LEFT: *Sleeping Houses 18* (2012), *Sleeping Houses 13* (2009), *Sleeping Houses 14* (2012), *Sleeping Houses 19* (2012)

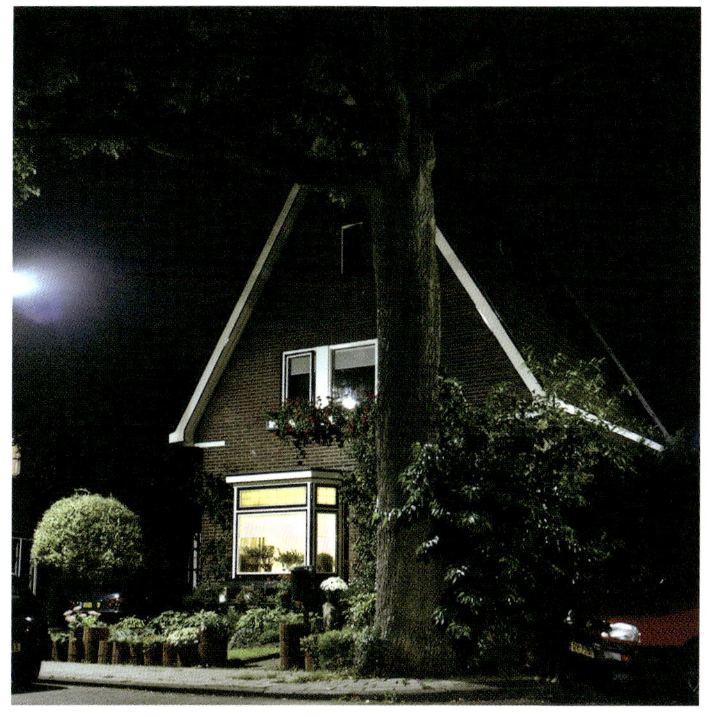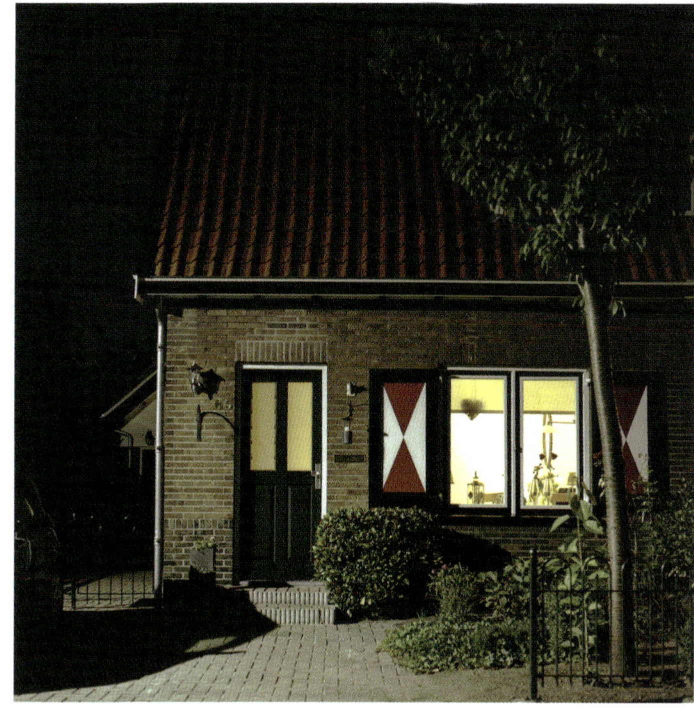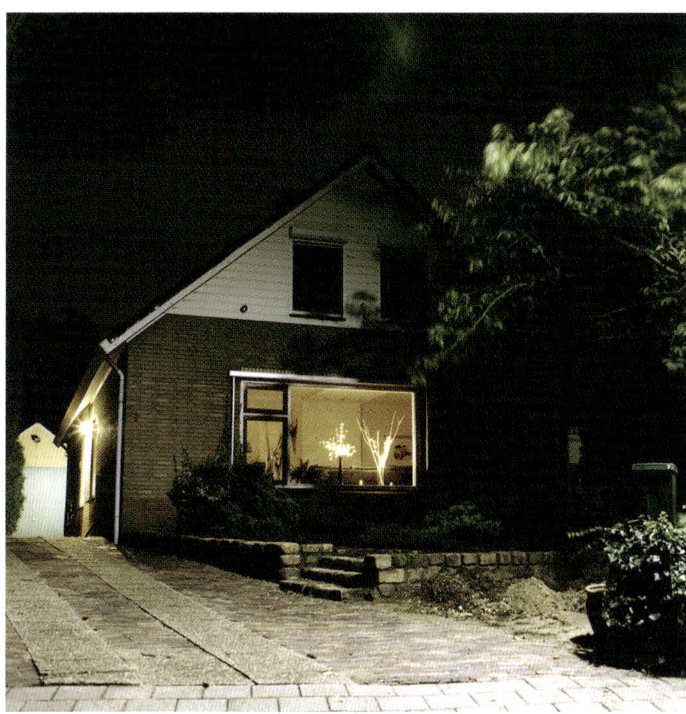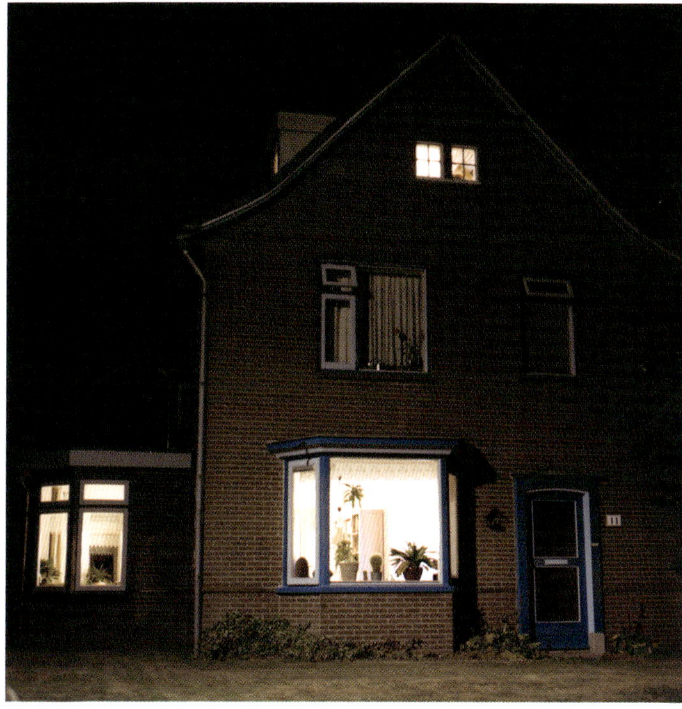

STEICHEN FOR STEHLI

BY **BRIAN SHOLIS**

As it steamed across the Atlantic one day in 1926, the *Isle de France* was the site of a chance encounter. Ruzzie Green, at the time an illustrator and designer, was on his way to Europe, perhaps to the Swiss headquarters of the Stehli Silks Corporation, where he served as art director. On deck he chanced upon Edward Steichen, the artist whose pictures were revolutionizing fashion photography. The two struck up a conversation, and, in short order, a deal: Steichen would contribute designs to Stehli's popular "Americana" line of fabrics. The fruits of their collaboration, when released to the public the following spring, would prove to be not only a commercial success, they would draw together a remarkable number of aesthetic, social, and economic trends: celebrity, artistic abstraction, mass production and consumption, the creative appropriation of everyday consumer objects—in short, much of what we identify with modern American society and culture.

Green and Steichen's meeting came at an auspicious moment. Historians of American culture, including Lizabeth Cohen and William Leach, have described the mid-1920s as an era of standardized production, mass consumption, corporate expansion, and increasingly influential advertising. America had emerged from the wreckage of World War I relatively unscathed and the stock market crash was still a few years away. Five-cent theaters featuring ethnic films were losing ground to the Hollywood system; mom-and-pop shops were being displaced by department stores and national chains. Recognizable brands were being promoted by familiar names and faces.

Stehli's "Americana" line capitalized on these transformations, deploying celebrity name recognition to sell its mass-produced textiles. Green hired nearly a hundred prominent figures to create—or at least lend their names to—these patterns, which were sold by the yard for dressmaking and other domestic applications. Participants included Helen Wills, an eight-time Wimbledon champion, the cartoonist John Held, Jr., and the fashion designer Pierre Mourgue.

Green commissioned dozens of artists to create modernist patterns for Stehli, but Steichen was the only photographer who contributed to the "Americana" line. His popularity among fashion cognoscenti and his willingness to collaborate with others made him a natural fit for the endeavor. Already recognized for his talents, he had returned to New York in 1922 and was soon hired as the chief photographer at Condé Nast. Working in collaboration with Nast and Edna Woolman Chase, Condé Nast's top editor, Steichen had introduced the clarity and clean lines of photographic modernism to a field still in thrall to the soft-edged Pictorialism of his predecessor, Baron Adolphe de Meyer. Steichen was committed to joining the visual language of modern art to commerce, and would, in addition to his work for Stehli, design glass for Steuben and pianos for Hardman, Peck, and Company.

As with the creative collaborations that characterized his magazine work, in making his textile patterns Steichen built upon experiments Stheli's art director Ruzzie Green had attempted himself. Gathering together small-scale common objects—sugar cubes, mothballs, carpet tacks, beans and rice, and the like—Steichen arranged them into grid-like patterns on a seamless backdrop. It was through his artistry, in particular his ability to control dramatic lighting, that Steichen turned these objects into semi-

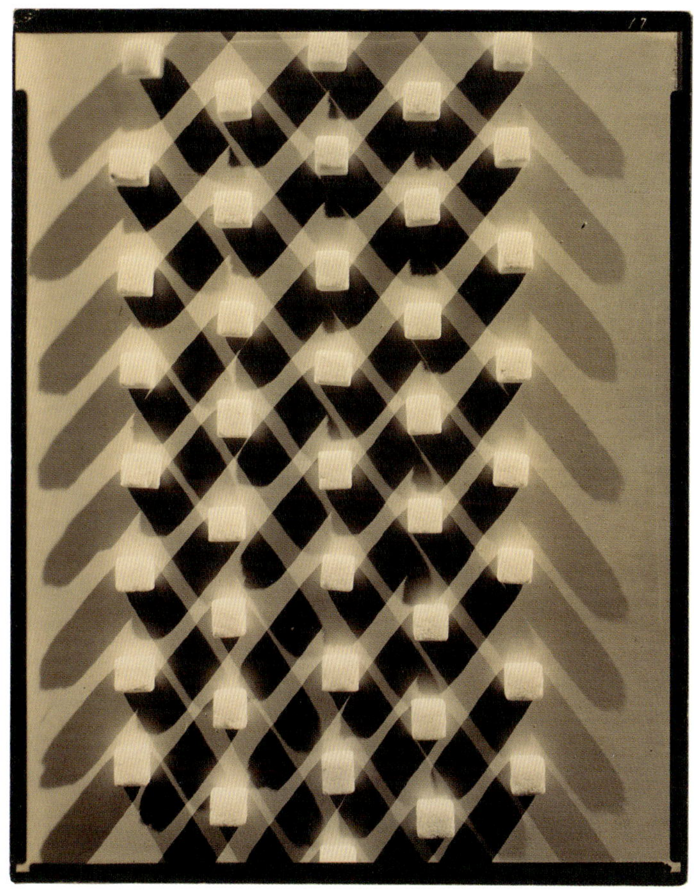

Sugar Cubes: Design for Stehli Silk Corporation (1926–27)

abstract patterns that, he felt, were "justifications of the Machine Age." They were successful as commercial products, yes, but he also believed they were successful as art—that the force of his attention elevated these pedestrian goods and encouraged others to see in them similar aesthetic qualities. Steichen would thank Green for opening up a new way of working, writing on the back of a photographic print: "To Ruzzie … for opening up this beautiful opportunity into a new field of photography. This sounds pompous, but 'taint meant that way."[1]

Indeed, Green, or someone else at the Stehli Silks Corporation, understood Steichen's achievement and donated samples of his textiles to the Metropolitan Museum of Art the year they were produced. Looking at the fabrics now, it's easy to see why. These angular compositions of small, geometrically shaped objects have an Art Deco flair, and Steichen wasn't afraid to break the rhythm of the grid if it added dynamism to the overall composition. He lowered his spotlights to table level, causing nearly flat objects to cast shadows, thereby broadening the tonal range of the photographs and adding further variety to the compositions. Stehli then printed these patterns in a number of color combinations. A grid of sugar cubes appears first in navy, tan, and sea-foam green, then in brown, olive, and lavender; an arrangement of coffee beans and rice appears in bright red, pink, and black, or in turquoise, deep blue, pink, and green; a swirling pattern of buttons and thread was printed in at least six different color combinations.

"My motivating impulse as a photographer is purely objective," Steichen asserted in July 1927. "Unless this effort, when achieved, can reach people, it will be dead. It must gain its vitality by being projected into the lives of man, and this is being brought about through the use of modern mechanics, in short, through industrialism."[2] Steichen, in collaboration with Green, was using technology to distribute photography through new avenues. Today, new, inexpensive printing technologies like Print All Over Me and Zazzle are allowing a new generation of artists to mass-produce and distribute their images on clothing. And an altogether different cohort of photographers is returning to the craft of studio experimentation to make abstract compositions and other formal experiments that Steichen himself would celebrate.

It's easy to comprehend the artfulness of Steichen's pictures, and the textiles created from them. What's harder to appreciate now, and what remains radical about this collaboration, is just how popular Steichen's creations were and how unusual they were for their time. Thousands of women across the country bought fabrics featuring semi-abstract arrangements of rice and beans or carpet tacks, then turned them into dresses. Such engagement by the public was enabled by Green's twin observations: that women's taste was increasingly sophisticated, meaning that "conventional florals and polka-dots" could be left behind; and that artists were increasingly aware that there was "drama in the American scene which could be given a wider expression." No artist working for Stehli would give better expression to this drama than Steichen.

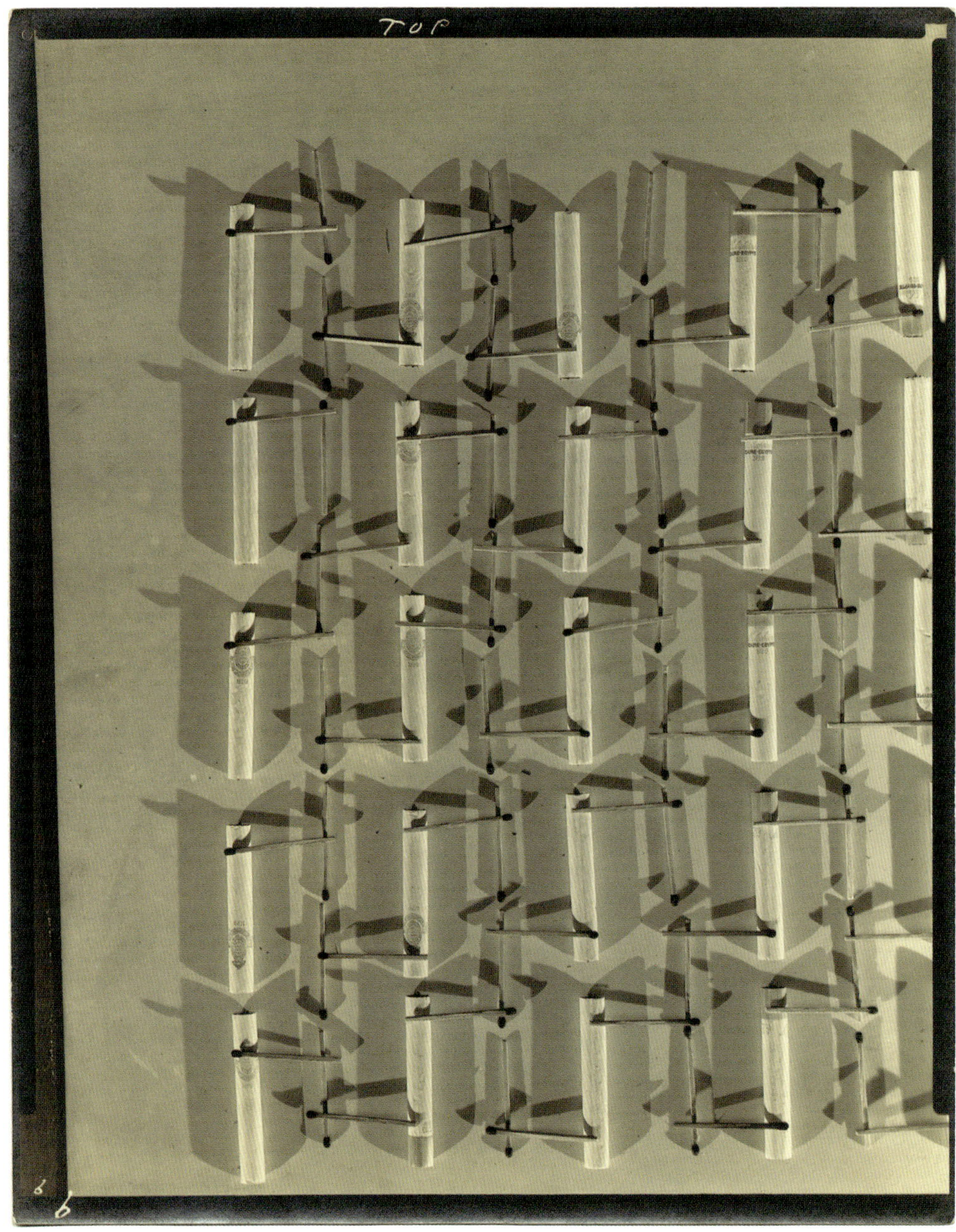

Cigarettes and Matches: Design for Stehli Silk Corporation (1926–1927)

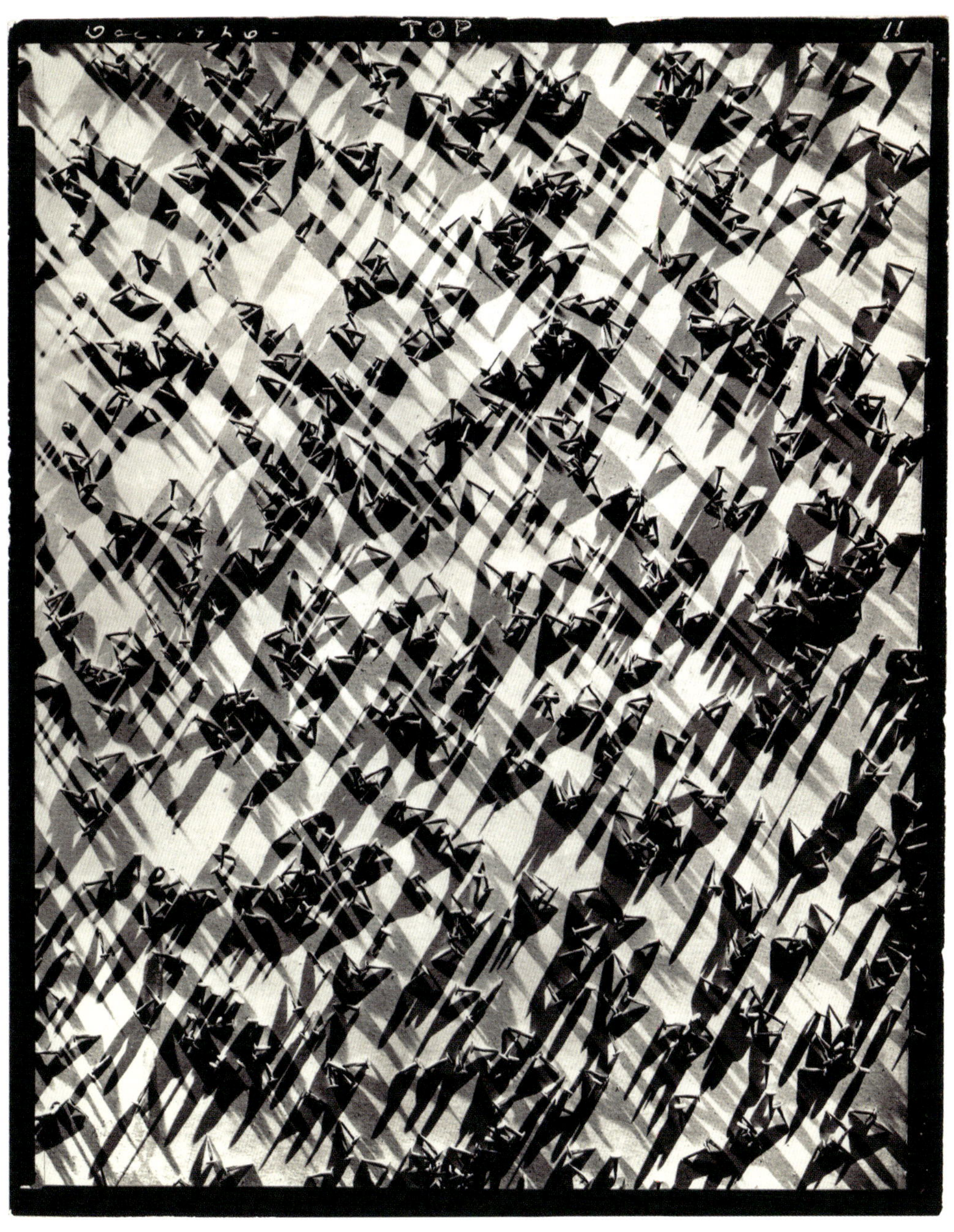

Tacks: Design for Stehli Silk Corporation (1926)

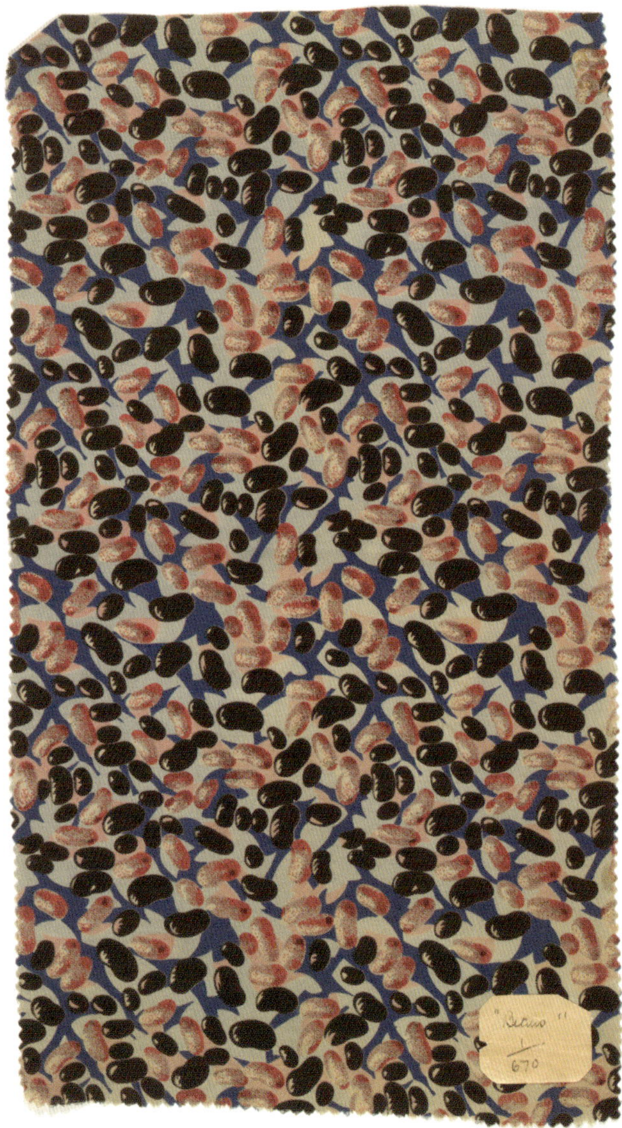

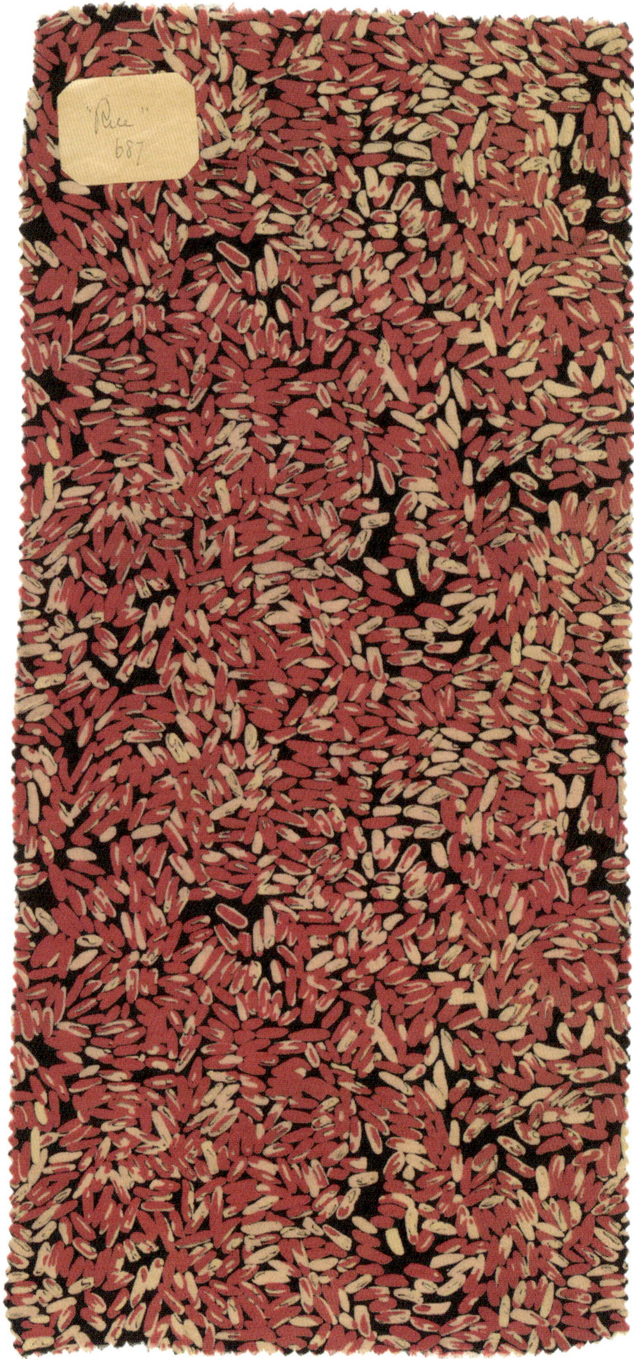

THIS PAGE: *Beans Stehli Silk Design* (c. 1927), *Rice Stehli Silk Design* (c. 1927)

44   OPPOSITE: Various ephemera, Stehli Silk Corporation

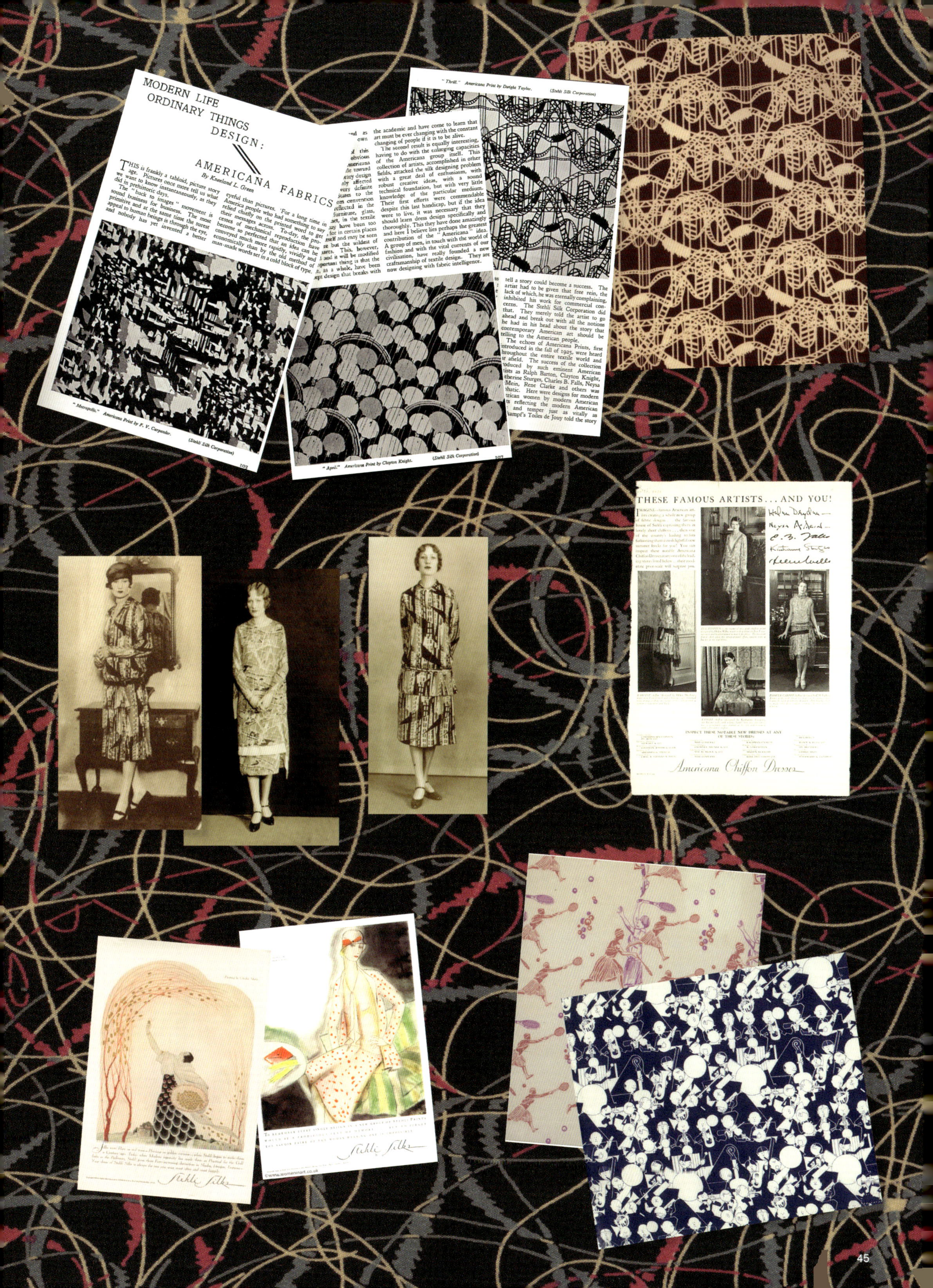

COLIN SNAPP
NV REGIONAL

NV Regional, filmed at Hoover Dam, on the border between Arizona and Nevada, is a ninety-minute, single-channel digital video capturing the constant stream of tourists as they traverse a terraced walkway. Their single goal is to reach a viewpoint adjacent to the dam, where presumably they will take pictures and return, traveling along the same route in reverse. Many do, in fact, carry cameras.

In the visual narrative, animated figurative shadows of the visitors vary over the course of the day according to the sun's path, which is the only detail in Snapp's film that embodies difference. The seemingly endless procession of people plodding up and down steep switchbacks appears to be in an otherwise desolate location. Without the sun to indicate time of day this durational situation remains entirely atonal.

As we watch the video, an incessant hum in the background becomes evermore distinct. The sound is recorded noise emitted from power lines located at the parking lot of the visitor center; it is the score to this journey. The production stills from *NV Regional* featured in this issue of *OSMOS Magazine* demonstrate a determined repetition inherent to the managed site, as well as the effect of repetition as a conceptual devise employed by the artist.

Absent this information however, the travelers in their surroundings appear otherworldly, like religious disciples on a desert pilgrimage. Like much of Colin Snapp's work, *NV Regional* acts to transform key destinations within America's middle class from the mundane to the monastic.

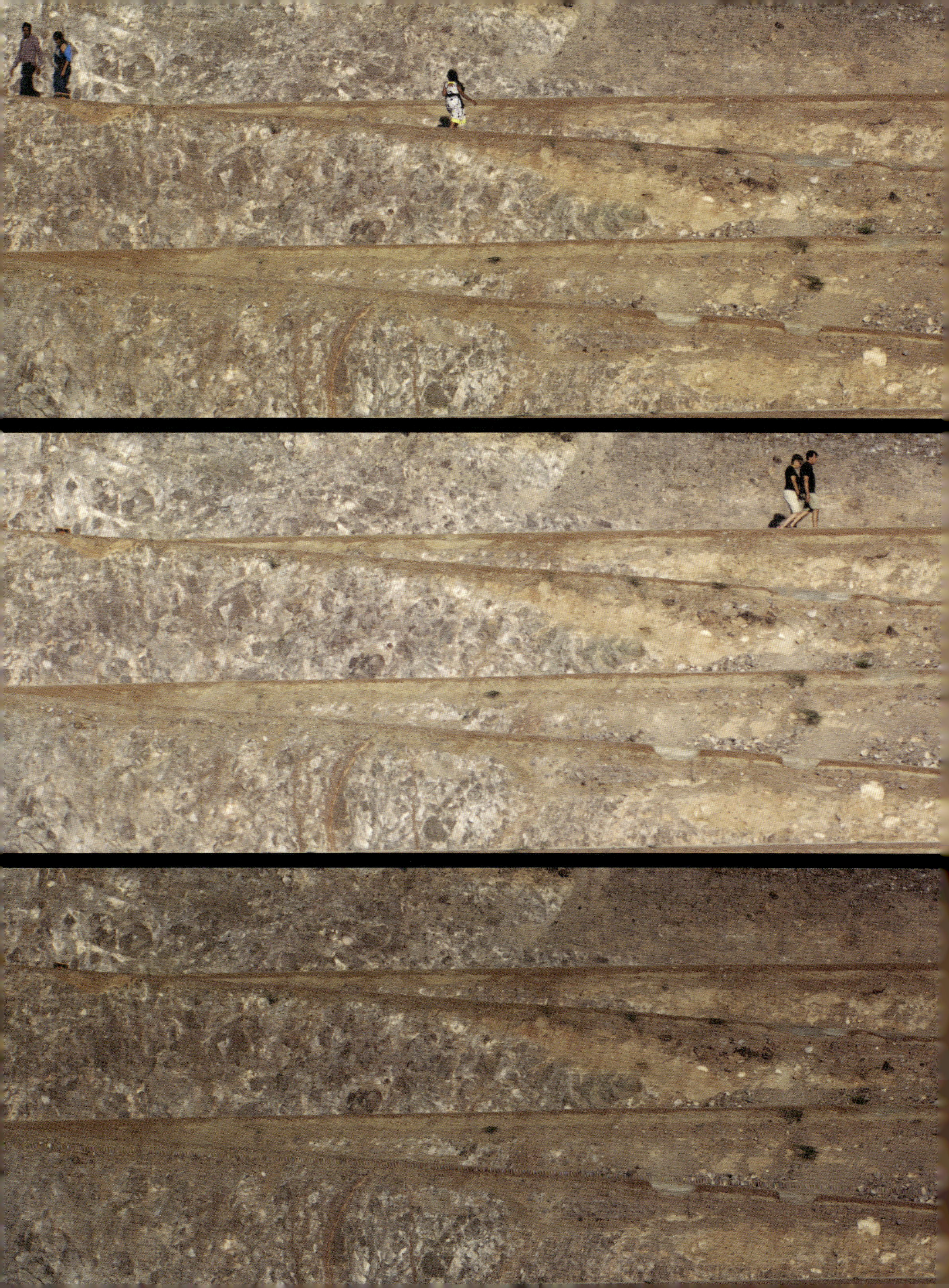

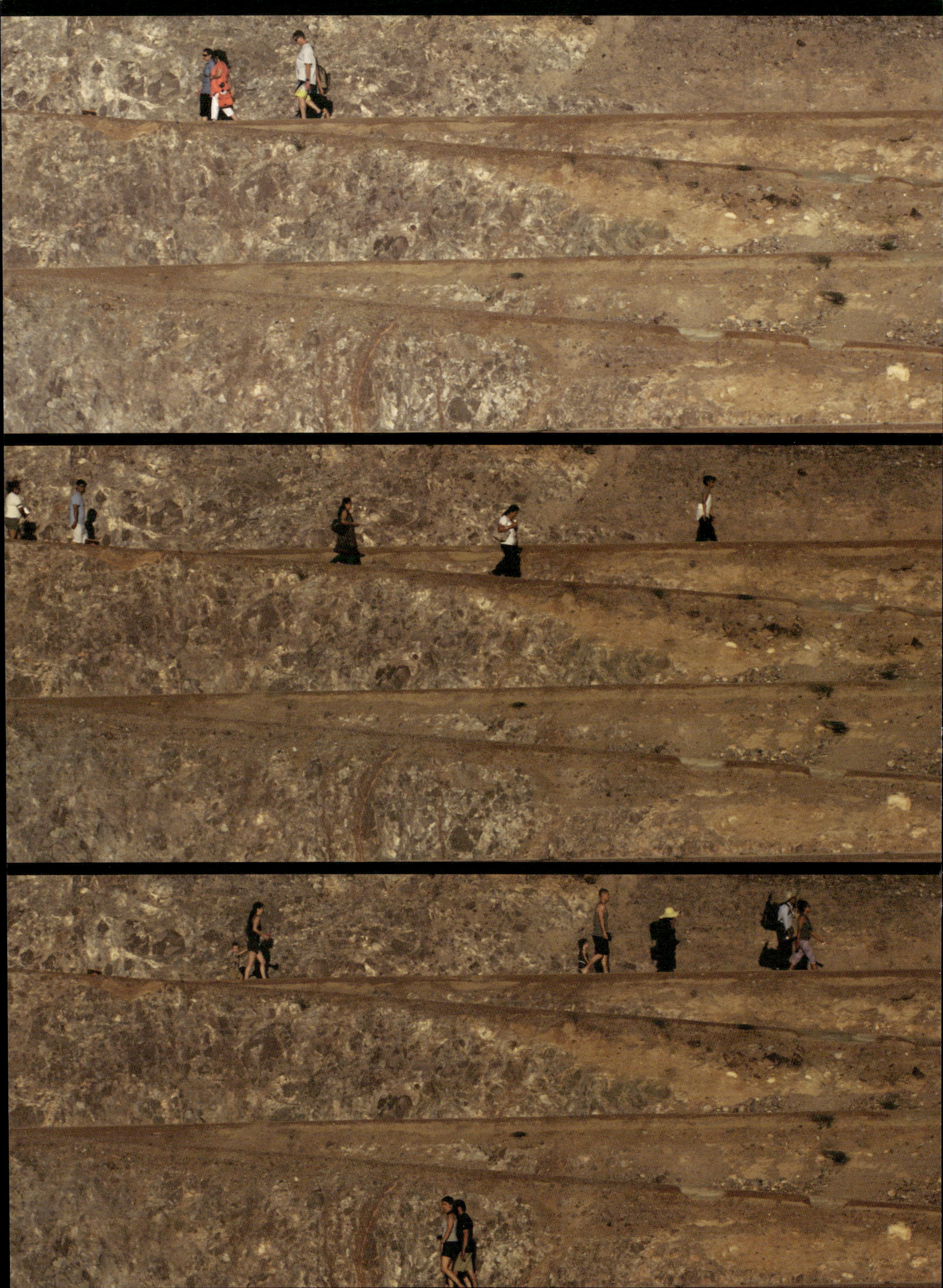

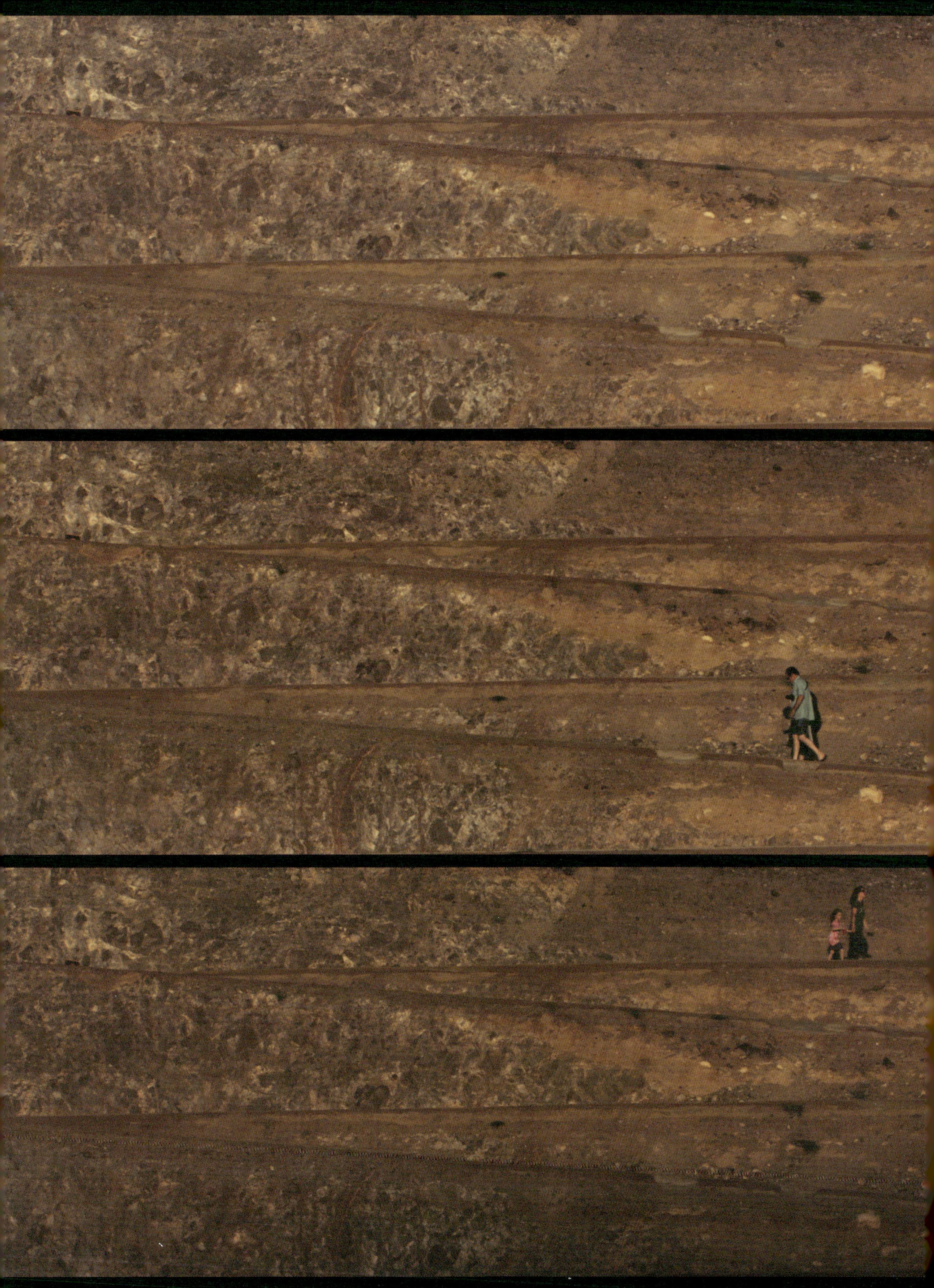

Andrea Arrubla: Lovesick Drawings

On the second floor of a three-story building on Avenue A, three blocks from the offices of OSMOS, Bruce High Quality Foundation University established the temporary headquarters of their artists' residency program. En route one evening last May to buy beer and chips at the corner grocery, a sign advertising open studios beckoned. We let ourselves into the building and climbed the steep staircase to find a single artist (and two cats indulgently making paw prints on the artist's drawing table). We seemed to be the only visitors, but from the uncertainty of our grounds for entering the studio and our unease about the sudden attention we each required of each other under newly installed fluorescents, a tender visit emerged when Andrea Arrubla presented us with a series of drawings on newspaper she had begun just days before. A few days later, Andrea came to an opening at OSMOS Address. Our interest in the drawings intensified as the conversation continued and the relationship evolved.

When we asked Andrea to describe the drawings for this issue of *OSMOS Magazine*, she wrote: "*Lovesick Drawings* is a project that bloomed out of a relationship that coincided with my first day at the BHQFU 2014 Summer Residency. Although drawing is an unusual medium for me to work with, I was inspired to use the surface of the *Brooklyn Rail*'s Art Criticism in Europe issue, as I was personally experiencing the impact of the female figure and its variations. This served as a way to blend in my personal celebration as well as highlight the constant problematic of female representation in the art world." BY CAY SOPHIE RABINOWITZ

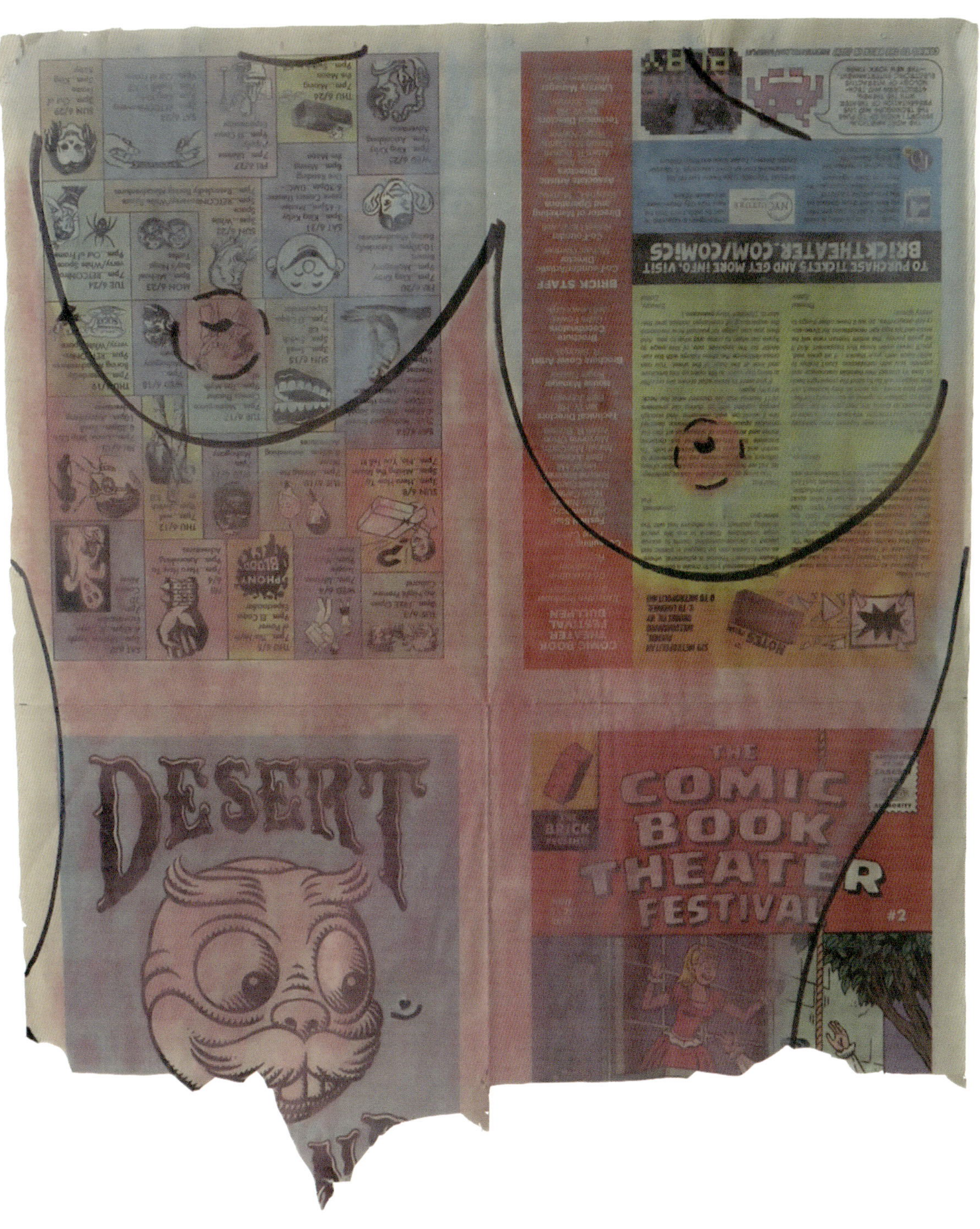

Lovesick Drawing 10 (2014)

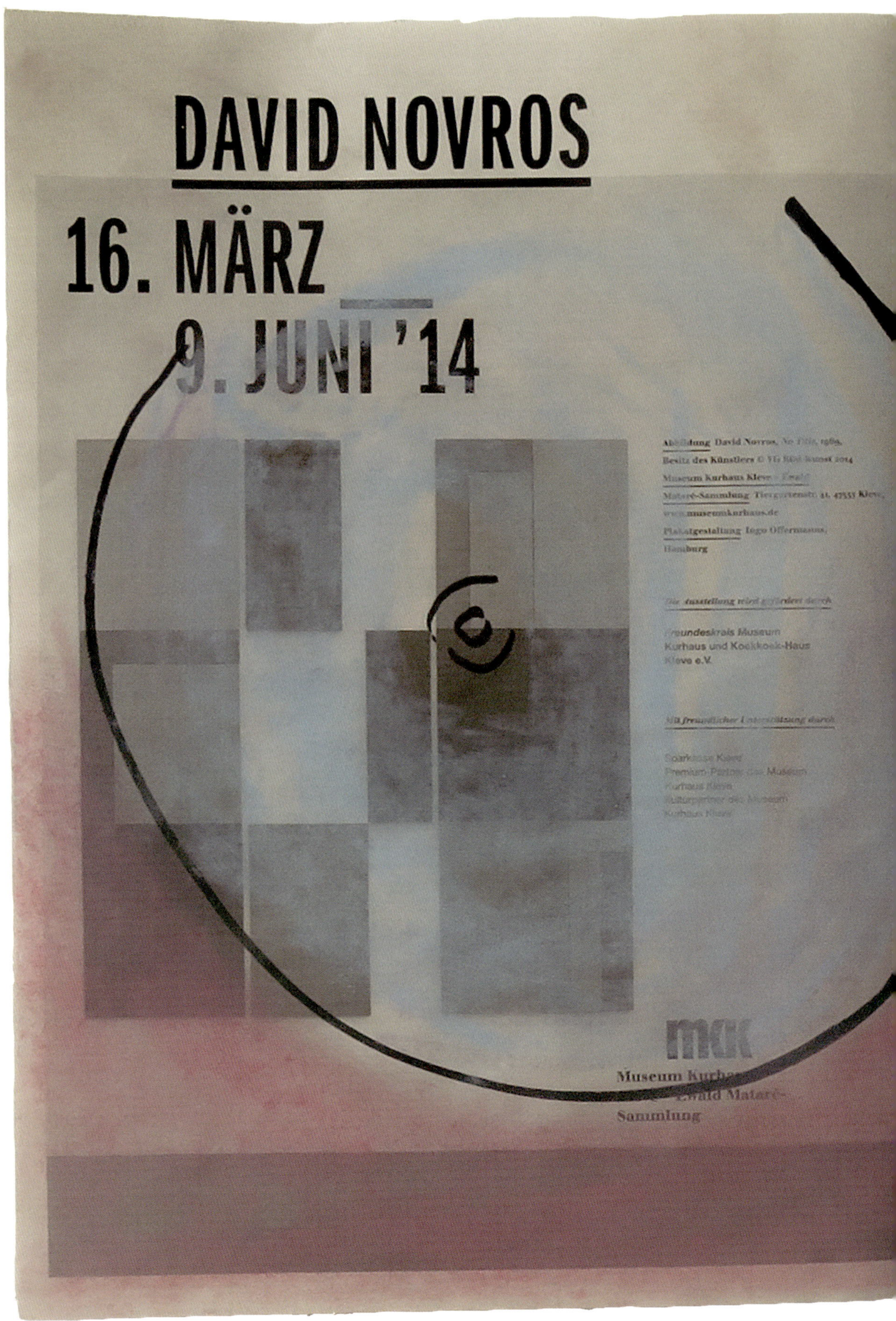
DAVID NOVROS
16. MÄRZ
9. JUNI '14

from *Miransù* by Monica Sarsini

TRANSLATED FROM THE ITALIAN BY MARYANN DE JULIO

to my grandmother Isabella

What a bad feeling, an indescribable thing. Nothing hurts me. I feel overwhelmed, my breathing, it seems like the world is collapsing on me. Maybe I miss your grandfather, maybe I miss him. Good God, it's too much that he's dead, everyday more. I was used to not having any worries, that's not such a small [illegible]. Without the worries I felt more secure. It's now I feel in danger. Loredana's right when she says you have so much stuff to sell if it came to that. It's not that I'm afraid of starving to death. It's that I don't know why this continual anguish. I feel unhappy, truly. Your grandfather made me live like a monk so that we could put together these pennies. I put them with him too. It should all be mine. Your aunt's husband came to Italy with a handful of jewels. It wasn't such precious stuff, the amethysts are very cheap, I don't think there were diamonds. That's how he began to have debts, and your aunt paid them. He always says, you only like [illegible]. Your father is a lazzerone and I like him just the same. I can't have him in the house because they forbid me, your mother doesn't want it, end of story. He ruined everything, but each one does as he thinks best, I knew him as a boy, it's for that.

I would have wanted to be present when my father's [illegible] was violated so that I could make every effort to ease his pain in the soft hollow of an embrace. August 1944 the Germans vacated the hills of Florence, where they had stationed the cannons. Behind the hills the allied army, Indians, English, New Zealanders, Australians, Americans, which were part of the first line, my father [illegible] without exposure. From the terrace of his house, before feeling the blow, my father saw the smoke from the [illegible] then felt on his head the whistle of the projectile racing in the sky to explode on the enemy army. [several lines illegible]

neckerchiefs run up, then he went back in the house, up to his room and stretched out on the bed to read that book that had always amused him, but this time he didn't laugh, and he was upset, and didn't understand why. I would like to have been there to embrace him, just as he embraced me when they killed his son and my brother, to hold hidden in my lap the neck of a little boy whose carefreeness has been devastated, instead I was not yet born, my family of men wounded in life. Those two on bicycles were never made to confront the pain that they caused, just as the son of the contadino who killed my brother did not come to be sorry, not even when grown up, even if he hadn't done it on purpose, I, as well, if I hadn't done it on purpose must apologize if at table I spill my glass full of water on the tablecloth, and these men that killed, violated the joy of a child, frightened his existence, that fixed forever in a precise moment the unfolding of his time, continued to live without feeling the necessity of begging pardon from the bright eyes of my father as a boy, I knew from his look that for his whole life he has tried to run from that day.

I can't be happy. And I don't need anybody to take care of me, I can take care of myself! Your aunt's husband always wants to be right, he fancies himself better than Schuffer, the head of the hospital, professor of anatomy. He was expelled, he was an antifascist. That fool of a brother of mine, with two others more fool than him, one became a municipal doctor, the other no, he was his own signorino, he had a private practice, when the students collectively decided that no one should stand up to applaud him at the last anatomy lesson he said, what does politics have to do with a bravissimo professor who has taught us anatomy in a marvelous way, we know everything about the human body now, I stand up and clap my hands. They had told him not to do it, and when the professor left him and these other two fools stood up and began to clap their hands. Then they beat them up, if you had seen the marks on my brother's body! When he got out of prison I welcomed him with open arms, he was a pediatrician, if they telephoned him at night because a baby was about to die he ran even in pajamas with the greatcoat on his back, all the people adored him, true communists as they say. All the wars that there were he fought in them. The Germans took him at Rodi and they brought him to Germany. He escaped because working in the hospital together with him there was an Austrian who at a given moment understood that Germany was finished. So he said, Doctor, let's leave, Germany is kaput, and they escaped. He was a medic, not a doctor, always with his little stars, his grade of Italian lieutenant, in the winter the Germans had offered him one of those tents that they had, and he refused it. But he defended them too. In line they gave a bowl of boiled millet, the other prisoners rebelled, he said, but what are they supposed to do even they don't have anything to eat!

When he returned I sent your grandfather, they named him an antifascist, I told him, have mercy, you go and take him by the back roads, come with him here, there weren't any trains. He arrived among the first, the workers were walking to work. I wouldn't want something to happen then and there, I said, they'd killed your other grandfather a few days before even though he'd only done good to people; a couple of families were living in Paradiso, a disgusting place, full of people that were dying of hunger. They went to the shopkeeper to get something to eat and he paid the bill, no clothes, or other stories, but for eating he took care of it. Like my brother had done for the rest, being a pediatrician, he only treated children, he treated old people too but all in all children more than others. Those days there wasn't the Cassa Mutua like now, you needed the doctor, if there was no libretto di miserabilità. When he saw that someone without the libretto didn't do so many wonderful things, if they said to him

how much must you have to visit the child, he answered, but what do you mean, buy him a little meat broth and give it to him. It was the same with the Germans, we had lost trace of them, finally one day a letter arrives, after so much time. When it arrived it went to Aunt Cara's. It said, when I knew that you were all safe and sound I got on my knees and kissed the ground. It was emphatic, eh! When he and your grandfather appeared out of nowhere on the little bridge the workers were arriving, in droves, on foot, they would recognize him and, uhhh! Our doctor has come back home! He rushed back to work. His wife's people, owners of a pharmacy, immediately found him the position of country doctor! He'd been away from home three or four years, his son was born and he hadn't seen him at all, and my sister-in-law sent him to the countryside! She wasn't a bad person the poor thing, but she didn't know how to stand up for him, he was weak, she was weaker than him. That's how he knew her. He had to go, it was an ugly time right after the war. When the first Englishman appeared, with that contraption on his head with all that grass for camouflage, he wanted a chair to sit himself down, sit down, sit down, he was saying. He arrived in the road, as if it were from this sitting room to the garden, ten or so meters distance, and everybody around him. He opened a box full of chocolates, they were fine, not at all like our soldiers who were dying of hunger, like the Germans, the Germans had always taken them from hunger, and thanks to the Americans, the English and the French the Germans would have had a bite, they're not such a sensitive people! They brought him the chair and he began to hand out cigarettes. There were no cigarettes, there was no bread, there was nothing in Italy. He began to offer white bread, they made a white bread like what I eat myself now that I have no teeth, bread that always gets moldy. And your mother and your aunt were there on the little gate, and they were watching. I said, you don't go near that man because I'm telling you, you turn your faces away! We didn't need the English! We had something to eat.

They hear voices it's true, someone from close, far away, bodies of words racked between nests of whiteness-down that rest on the brambles, or it's a dog lamenting the lightness of a chain where the wall of a partition is cracked from the frost, but it's the guarded clamor from the paths that return. [several lines illegible] Thus suddenly rises a wind that comes from under my shoulders like a smooth transparent avalanche, a sheet with its reasons without accompaniment descend on its surface chessboard of swift thoughts going away. Perch head of a headstone that crops out of the grave, you also just rose from its earth and takes the road toward its heaven. I take refuge inside the twisted trunk of an olive tree in order to support myself on a branch, which as pure cortex attracts from the eday. In the wide valley for contemplating furtively why I put down roots now there's only the furled yellow of the falling trees that he used as a boy.

The *Raíl* is proudly running *Miransù* as a serial which began in the December/January issue and will continue through the spring.

MONICA SARSINI was born in Florence, where she has taught writing. She is also an artist [illegible]. Her stories, *Lanterne* (Le Lettere, [illegible]) and *Crocifissa, Coloratura and others: A collection of stories*, was published in English under the title of *Eruzioni* (Italica Press, 1999). In 2008 her poetic book *Alice nel paese delle domandine* (Le Lettere, 2008) [illegible]. She edited an anthology of writing by women from the creative writing workshop at San Gimignano prison, without *Firenze* [illegible].

MARYANN DE JULIO is a Professor in the Department of Modern and Classical Language Studies at Kent State University in Kent, Ohio.

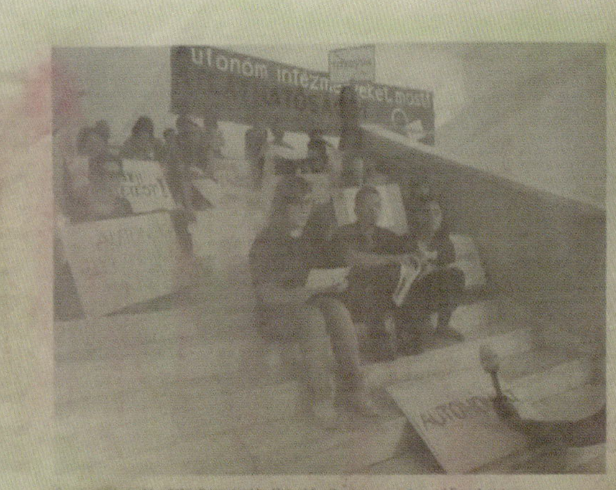

Occupy Ludwig, May 2013. Organized by United for Contemporary Art and Free Artists.

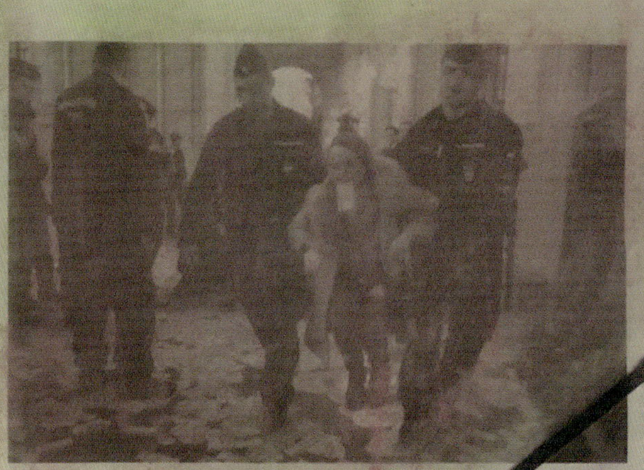

Raining Money at Vigadó, Budapest. Demonstration co-organized by Tranzit Action Group and Free Artists, March 14, 2014. Photo: Gabriella Csoszó / FreeDoc.

Hungary—A Post-Socialist Conflict Zone *by Edit András*

After the election in Hungary, carefully tailored to be favorable for the ruling party, nothing can stop FIDESZ, a conservative, right-wing party, from completing the creation of a retrograde, ethno-nationalist state-system with semi-feudal, semi-socialist features, the foundation of which had been laid down during the previous four years. The 2012 Democracy Index qualified Hungary as a "flawed democracy," however, on the basis of the latest measures of the government there is a good chance it will be downgraded into the category of "hybrid" or even "authoritarian regime," as it has happened with Putin's Russia, a regime close to present-day Hungary.

The populist rhetoric of the administration to complete the deconstruction of socialism is in sharp contrast with the sensation of déjà vu experienced by the people, who feel they are witnessing a return to "socialism with a national face" by means of a rapid, systematic removal of the basic institutions of democracy. Upward control, the main guarantee of democracy, is disregarded, as the final decisions are in the hands of the freshly re-elected Prime Minister Viktor Orbán in this centralized and highly controlled country. Following the fundamental changes in the constitution and in the political and economic spheres which will fortify the ruling party for decades, there have been transformations in education, art, and culture. The authoritative and systematic transformations assure state control in each and every segment of culture, eliminate transparency, and exclude participation.

From this situation, a culture war began, and is still going on.

The art scene here, especially in comparison to other post-socialist countries, has been quite apolitical for almost two decades. This is due to the mistrust of political art, and the stronghold of modernist and neo-avant-garde strategies. However, cultural politics have become divided along political and ideological lines, with the arbitrary measures of the regime lacking professionalism and favoring its own clientele, creating an over-politicized art scene. It is not possible anymore to step aside and ignore the political struggles and remain a neutral studio artist or idealistic critic. Culture was handed over to the Hungarian Art Academy (H.A.A.), a shadow ministry that has full power and authority to decide and administer public support for art and culture, including state subsidies. There is an option to gladly accept the boundless opportunities and financial support in exchange for sharing the dream of the leader of a conservative, Christian, and nationalist Hungary. But for those who wish to connect to the global art scene instead of the local, parochial one, and who have not yet left the country, the air is being sucked out of the room, and opportunities for making and exhibiting art are diminishing.

As the internationally acknowledged philosopher Miklós Gáspár Tamás rightly stated, contemporary Hungarian culture is not against the ideology of the recent administration, rather against its acts. Although there are artists who reflect the nationalist ideology, the cult of folk art, and the manipulation of history, the majority of advanced critical art is a kind of visual activism instead.

A grassroots organization against the empowerment of H.A.A. was initiated by the artists Szabolcs KissPál and Csaba Nemes. Curators, critics, and other artists joined them, and Free Artists was formed, whose first action was an intrusion into the meeting of H.A.A., demanding autonomy for arts. The process of replacing art professionals with commissars loyal to the ruling party to assure

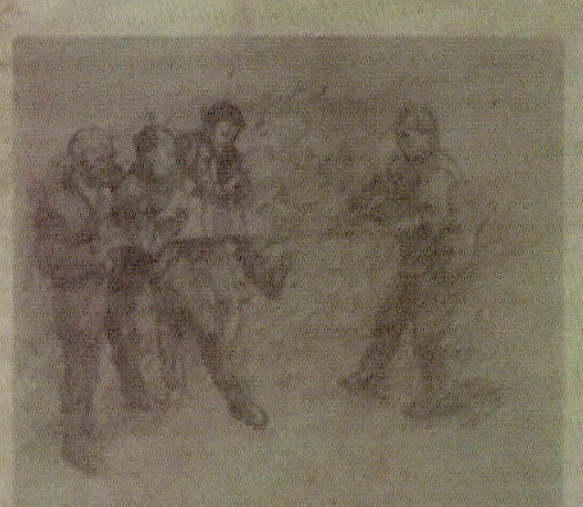

Drawing of an art student Peter Donka after the journalist photography (István Huszti) taken on the interruption of the first meeting of Hungarian Art Academy by Free Artists, at the moment when one of their representatives, Csaba Nemes, was attacked with a folder by a poet member of H.A.A. Dec. 2013. Courtesy of the owner of the drawing: Csaba Nemes.

self-censorship, neglecting open competitions at the Kunsthalle, and appointing the new director of the Ludwig Museum in Budapest in a non-transparent and orchestrated jury process have triggered new forms of visual activism. When the Kunsthalle was given to H.A.A., the young curators Márton Pacsika and Eszter Kozma along with their professor József Mélyi, a curator and respected critic, initiated regular actions and events outside of the building, called Outer Space, demonstrating against the invasion of an independent art institution by party politics. In response to the non-transparent process of appointing the director of the Ludwig Museum, the group United for Contemporary Art was established by the art and theory network tranzit.hu, and subsequently occupied the steps of the Ludwig Museum. The occupiers, comprising acknowledged artists, art historians, curators, and students, demanded complete transparency of the selection process, autonomy for cultural institutions, as well as dialogue between professionals and ministry officials. The most hard-core of the occupiers—including many members of the Free Artist group—were sitting, eating, sleeping on the steps, and organizing forums and events.

As part of the nation building, the rhetoric of the ruling party, based on the idea that the state socialist period was illegitimate and the previous government did not accomplish true political transition. The current administration picks up the political threads of 1944, as if a symbolic gesture would erase the period of state socialism and rewrite history. Thus, all the monuments connected to the democratic, liberal, or slightly leftist tradition are falling victim to the second wave of purification of public space, vulgar and commercial bronze figures, like "Girl with Dog," or depicting the television detective Colombo, are mushrooming in the city. Selective memory keeps only what are considered the "successful" events in Hungarian history in circulation. Failures or events demanding collective responsibility are not considered. The debate around the controversial monument to the German occupation of Hungary in 1944 in Budapest Freedom Square culminated around the time of the government election. According to the official government website, it will pay tribute to "all Hungarian victims with the erection of the monument commemorating the tragic German occupation and the memorial year to mark the 70th anniversary of the Holocaust." However, the protesters regard it a falsification of history, as it does not differentiate between the victims and the perpetrators and does not acknowledge the responsibility of Hungary in the Holocaust and World War II. On the designated place of the monument, a counter-monument, a living memorial was established. People put personal objects and stones there. The action was initiated by a small civil group including a few members of the Free Artists, András Rényi, an art historian and chair of the art history department of the Eötvös Loránd University, as well as the respected neo-avant-garde artist György Jovánovics. The process is still going on as I write this report. The fence erected around the construction site by the workers during the day is demolished by the protesters every evening.

Lovesick Drawing 3 (2014)

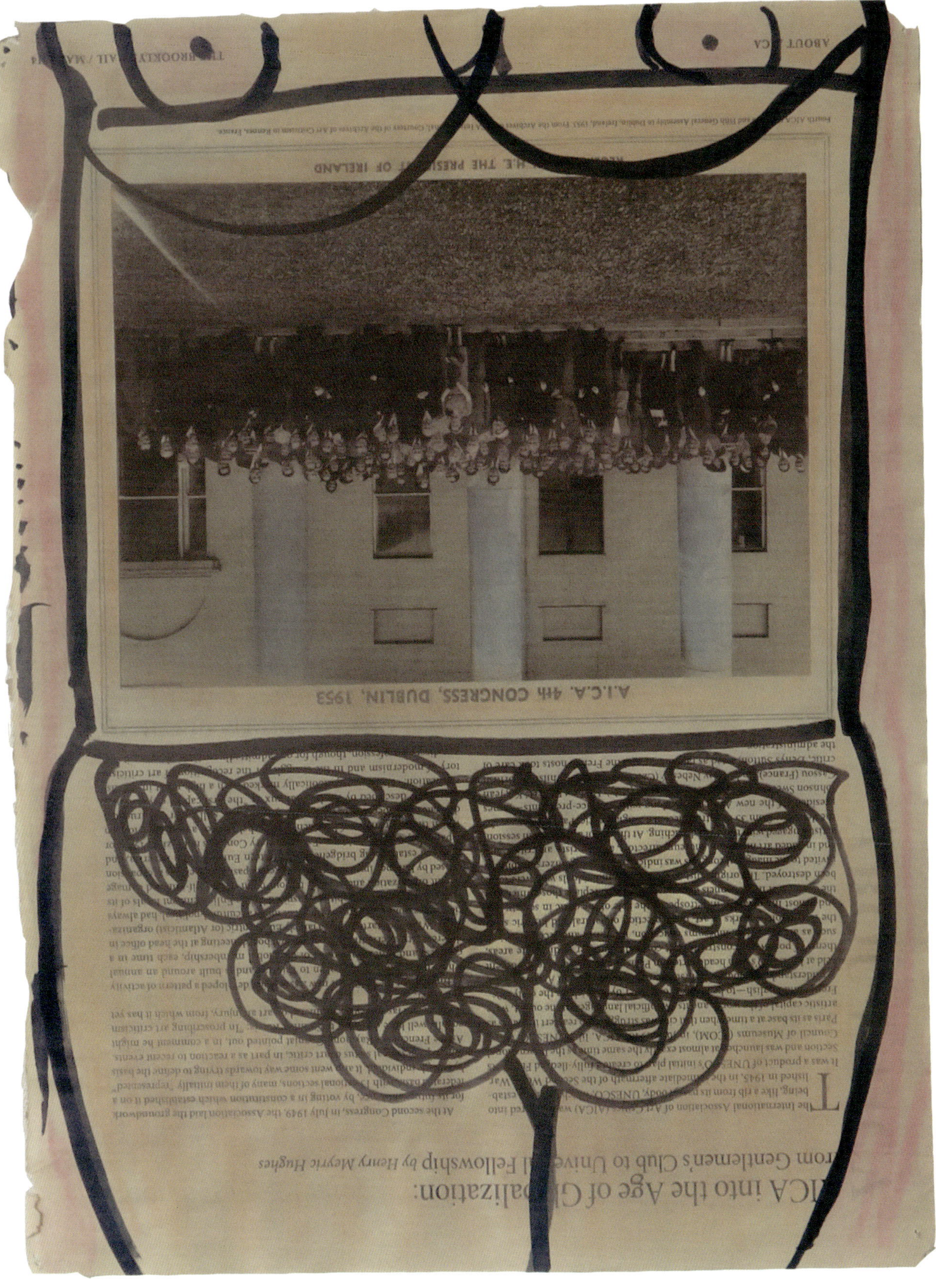

Lovesick Drawing 1 (2014)

JIŘÍ THÝN
FUNDAMENTAL ATTRIBUTES

How to make images in a context that is at once over-determined by the conventions of the avant-garde and oversaturated by contemporary visuality? The young Czech artist Jiří Thýn answers this question by continuously manipulating his frame of reference while maintaining a connection to the experimental studio practices of the Czech modernist tradition in which he studied. Meticulous dark room technique, baryta paper, and elaborately calibrated grayscales are employed to reexamine motifs often taken from Central European modernist structures—architectural and otherwise. Despite this rigorous and serious approach Jiří Thýn keeps up his enthusiasm for, or at least acceptance of, the markers of contemporary (art) world visibility and its cultural accoutrements.

Thýn's most recent series Consciousness as a Fundamental Attribute II (2014) brings together seemingly simple gestures: the entire series originates in the appropriation of pages from *frieze* magazine, which are cut, arranged on the studio table, and re-photographed. Pages with text and illustration of reviewed exhibitions and artworks mix with fashion advertisements. Thýn's incisions render these images artful in new ways, while additional ornamental elements such as round magnets strategically conceal details of the source images to underscore their materiality as torn and pinned printed matter.

The first cut, the primary attack on the integrity of the image in Thýn's hand, restores to it an urgency it may have lost in cultural circulation; he respectfully reinscribes it into a tradition of radical experimentation. The preposterous, un-ironic ethical demand of the titles of the works, *Consciousness as a Fundamental Attribute*, points back to the need to recognize and understand the noble basis and radical propositions at the heart of avant-garde artistic practice, even if it comes to us today as a regurgitated image in a monthly magazine.

Jiří Thýn was born in 1977 and studied at the Academy of Arts, Design and Architecture in Prague and at TAIK in Helsinki. He was a finalist for the Jindrich Chalupecky Award in 2011 and is represented by hunt kastner gallery in Prague, where he lives and works.

BY CHRISTIAN RATTEMEYER

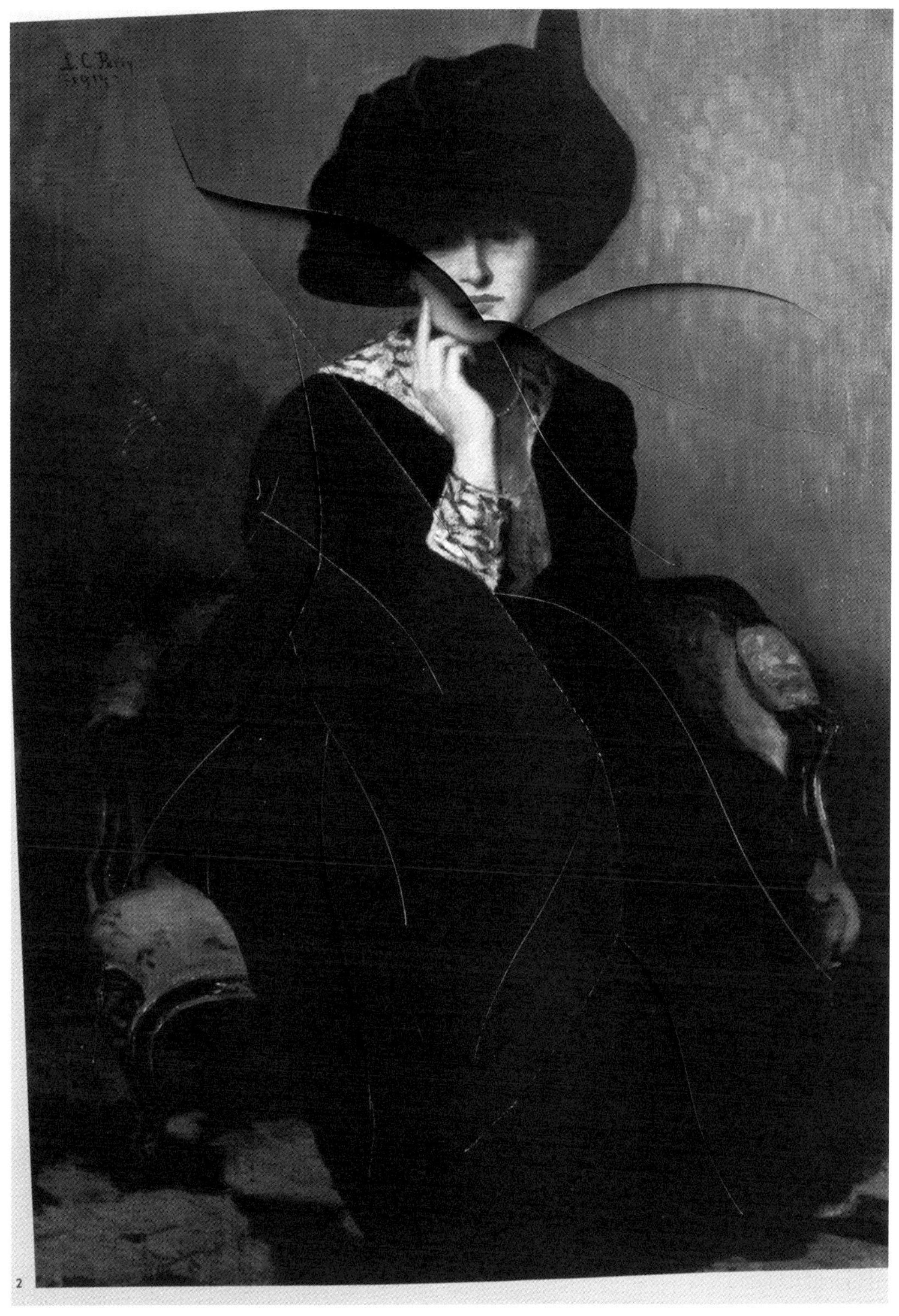

Consciousness as a Fundamental Attribute II (2014).
frieze, October 2013, issue 158, p. 212

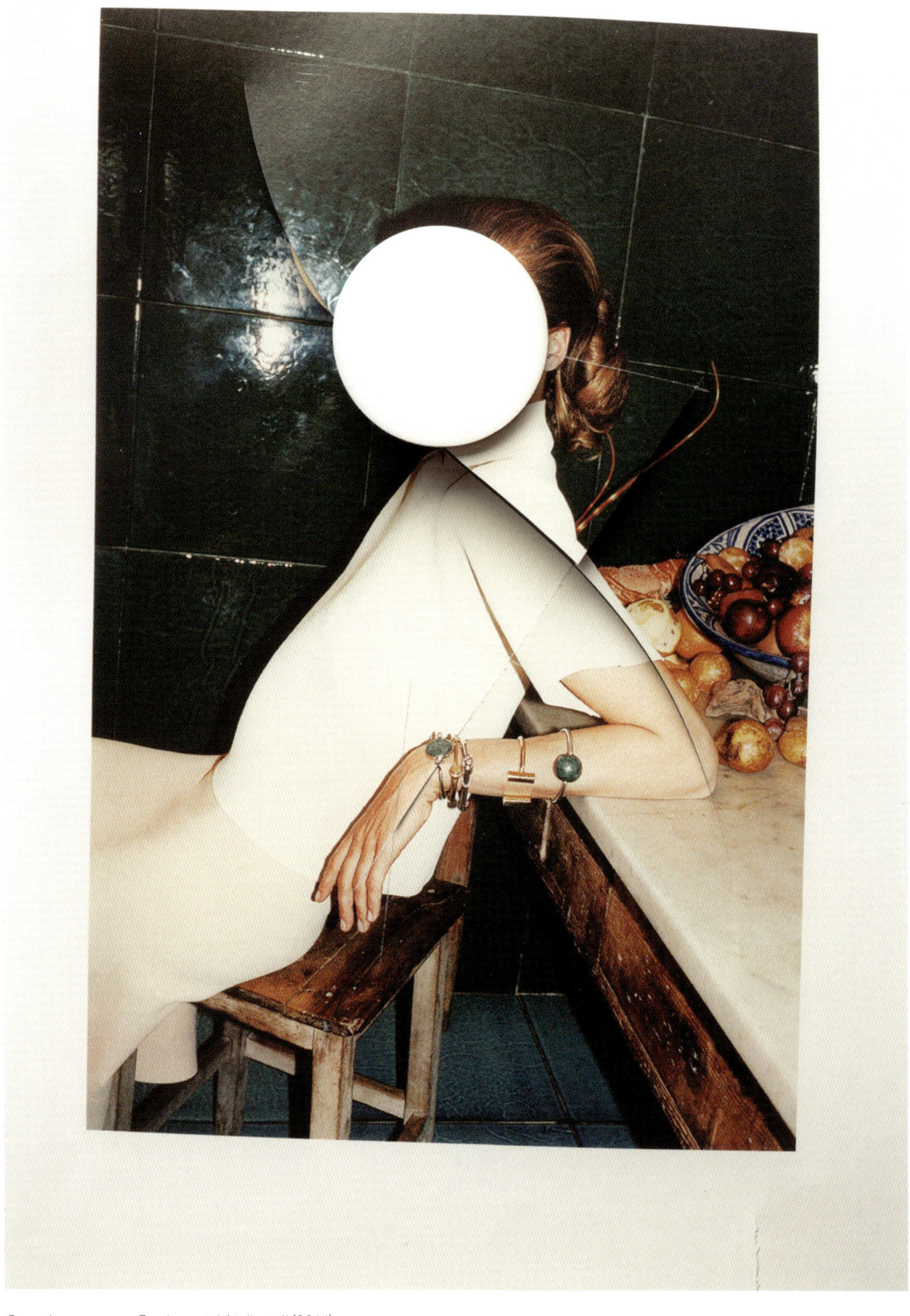

Consciousness as a Fundamental Attribute II (2014).
frieze, October 2013, issue 158

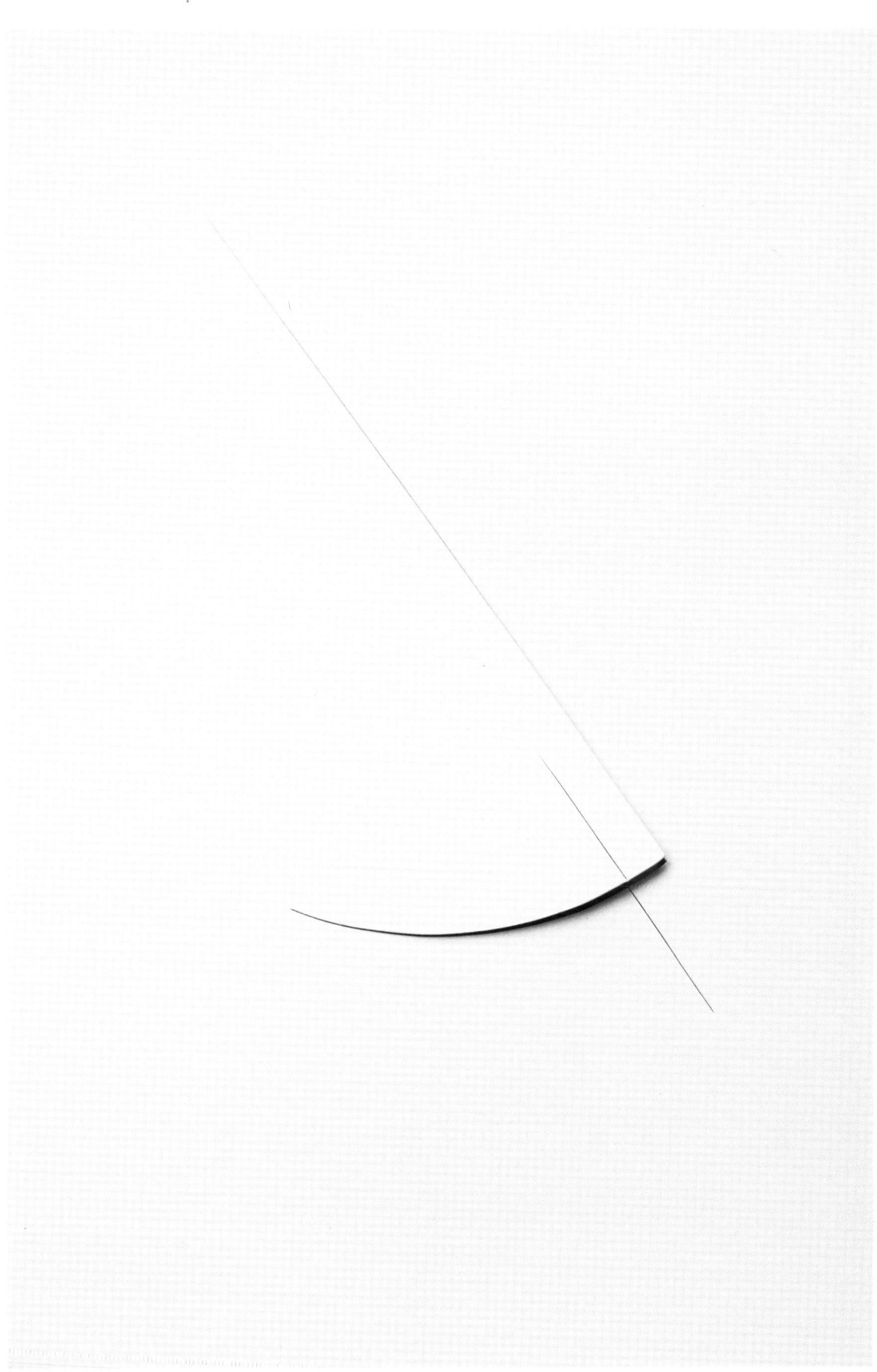

Consciousness as a Fundamental Attribute I (2013)

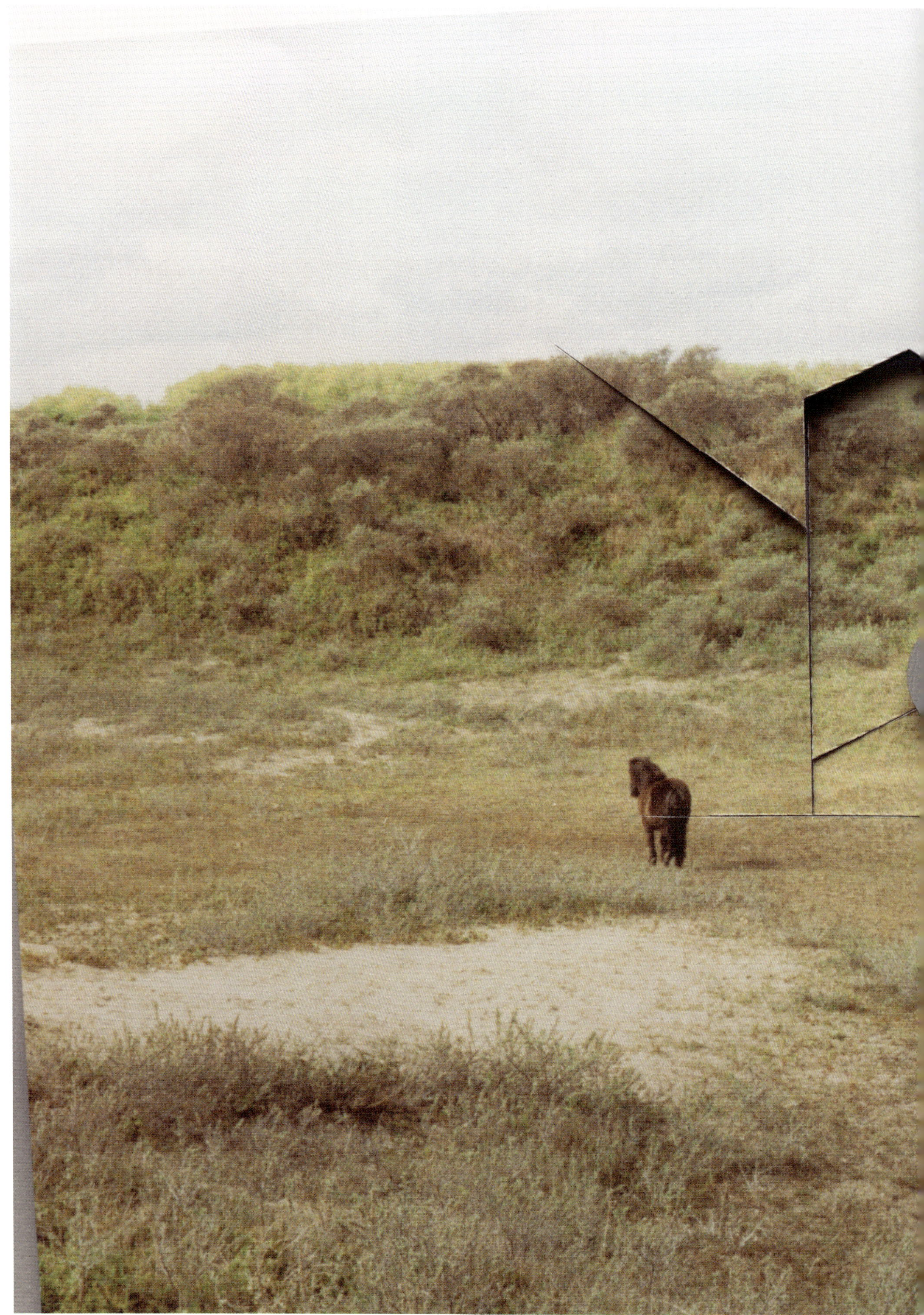

 Consciousness as a Fundamental Attribute II (2014). frieze, October 2013, issue 158

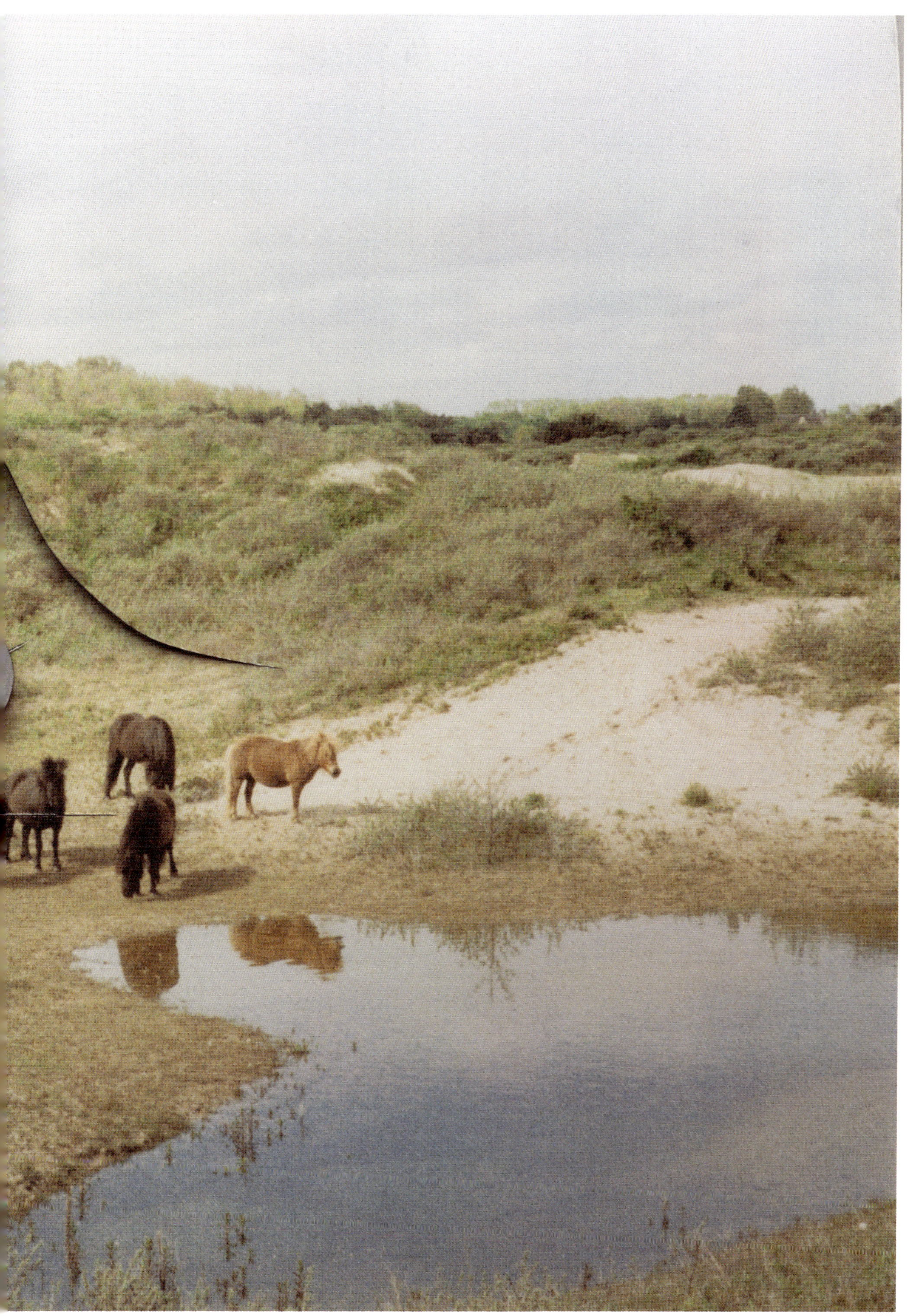

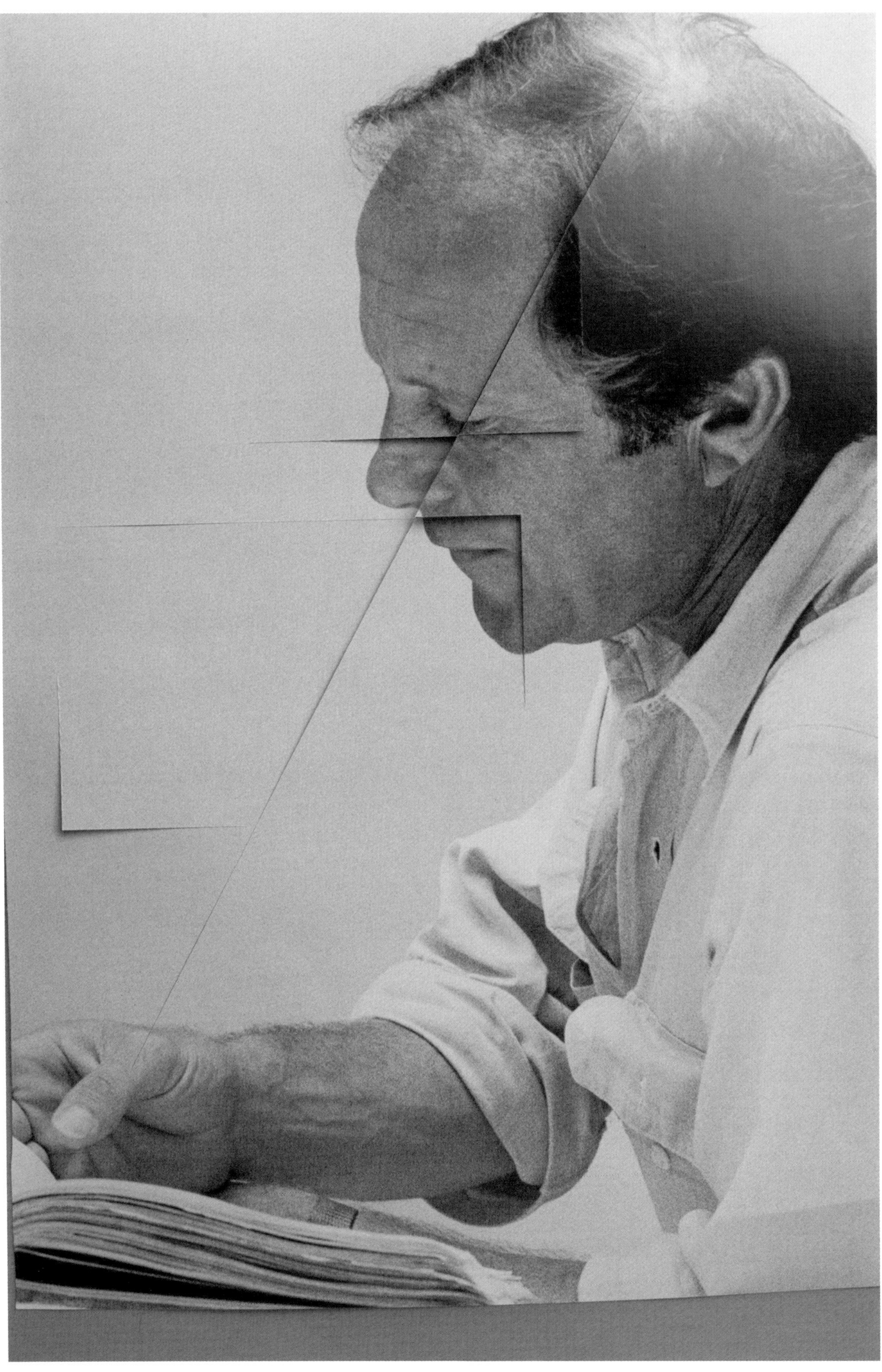

Consciousness as a Fundamental Attribute II (2014).
frieze, October 2013, Issue 158, p. 241

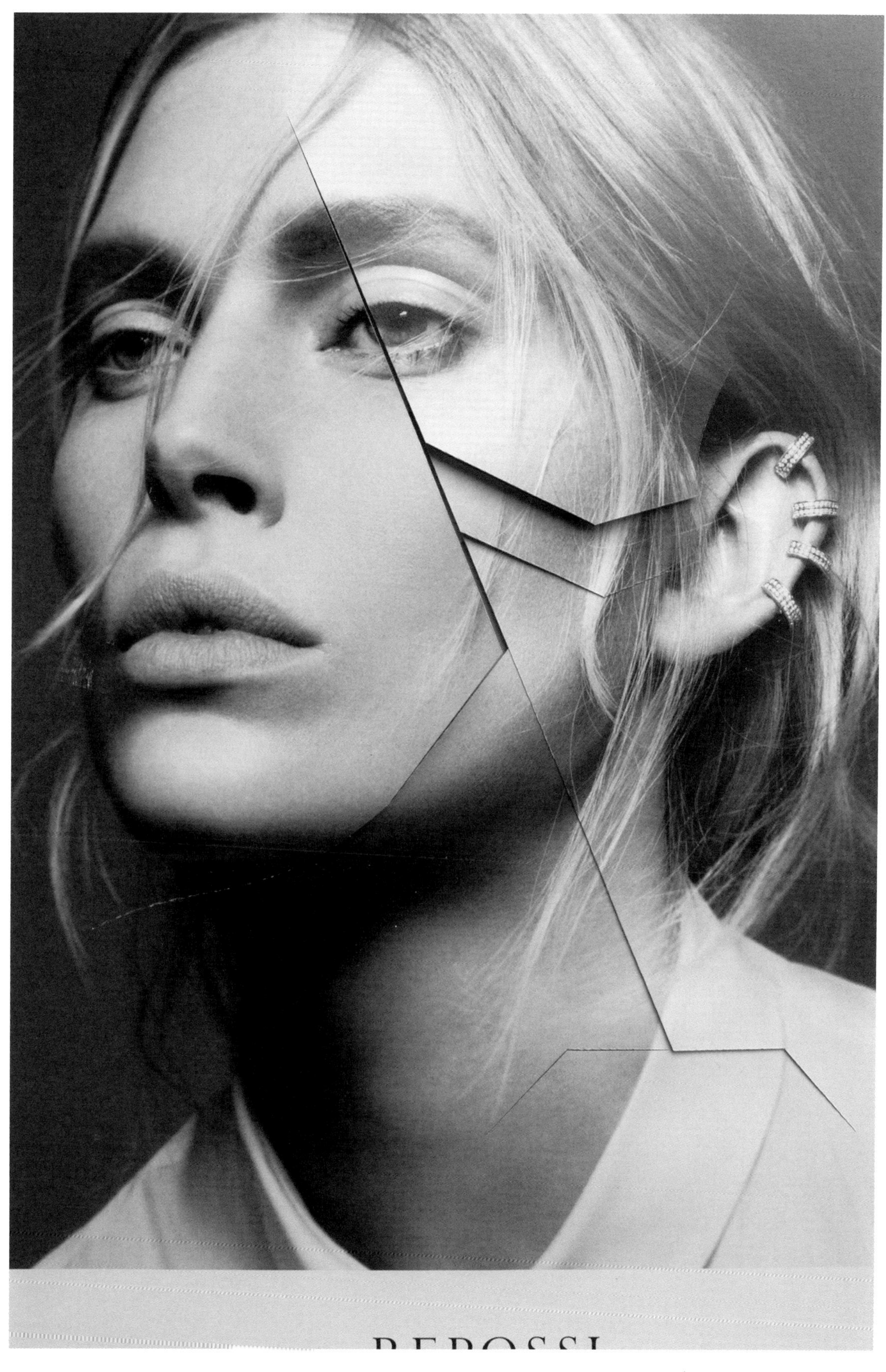

Consciousness as a Fundamental Attribute II (2014)
frieze, October 2013, Issue 158

#ISISfoodies

BY **LEON DISCHE BECKER**

Since their erasure of the Iraqi-Syrian border last June, ISIS has all but supplanted Al Qaeda in the Western imagination. We know a superior product when we see it—the Islamic State's apparatus makes bin Laden's nihilistic brainchild look altogether gauche. The distinction is particularly stark in the realm of public relations. While Al Qaeda's outreach was covert, mostly in Arabic, defined by it's late leader's handycam antics, ISIS has chosen a decentralized, open-sourced approach, encouraging individual fighters to develop their personal brands online. As a result, I have spent the past few months following dozens of foreign ISIS fighters on Twitter. These young men don't let American drones, Twitter's attempts to suspend their accounts, or their murderous day jobs prevent them from curating their virtual personas. Most of their content is in keeping with their reputation—Quranic proverbs alongside images of battlefield heroics and carnage. But not all is grim in the Islamic state. When they're not posting shots of severed heads and smiling martyrs, ISIS militants make a point of sharing light-hearted, banal comments and images—cat memes and food photography, in particular.

One of their favored edible motifs is Nutella. *The Wall Street Journal* called the images of militants posing with the popular breakfast spread "a deliberate strategy to make the Islamic State look more friendly and familiar to Westerners," while the *Daily News* understood "these bizarre, sugary images" as "attempt[s] to seem friendly and humane." But ISIS fighters who pose with Nutella aren't pretending to be normal people: in many ways, they are normal people: *everyone* loves Nutella. Moreover, as is well known throughout the Arab world, Islamic fundamentalists are foodies. They have a weakness for junk food, in particular, which makes sense given that it's one of the few indulgences permitted by a strict interpretation of Islam.

And while it's true that some of their food photography is intended to facilitate recruitment, the central message is not that ISIS fighters are "friendly and humane," but that they have an abundance of quality provisions, which may just be a prerequisite for luring other epicurean Jihadists their cause.

It's worth noting that there is nothing inherently humanizing, let alone bizarre, about these images. Rather, they will only appear that way to people who have unwittingly dehumanized the ISIS fighters (potential recruits, knowing their ideological brethren, won't make that mistake). While it may be convenient, in the face of a mounting campaign of ethnic cleansing, to stress these men's foreign- and otherness, that doesn't make it true. Of the reported thirty thousand men fighting for ISIS, an estimated two thousand grew up in the West, a hundred of them in the United States, and if we are honest, they are not that different from the other confused, young chauvinists among us. They, too, love Nutella.

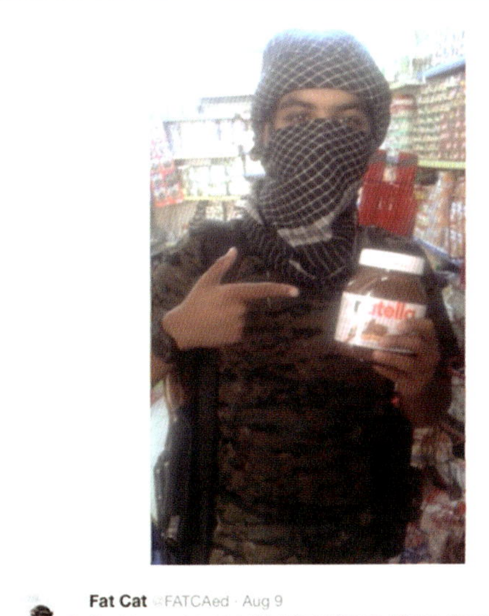

Fat Cat @FATCAed · Aug 9
Could an embargo on Nutella or Chupa Chups destroy the morale of #IS mercenaries? #ISIS (Nutella Halal ?)
pic.twitter.com/nZMBMyLEPC

3

Umm Irhab
@MuslimahMujahi1
Follow

Seriously the best ice cream here. Yacniiii....
Wasnt expecting this kind of jihad

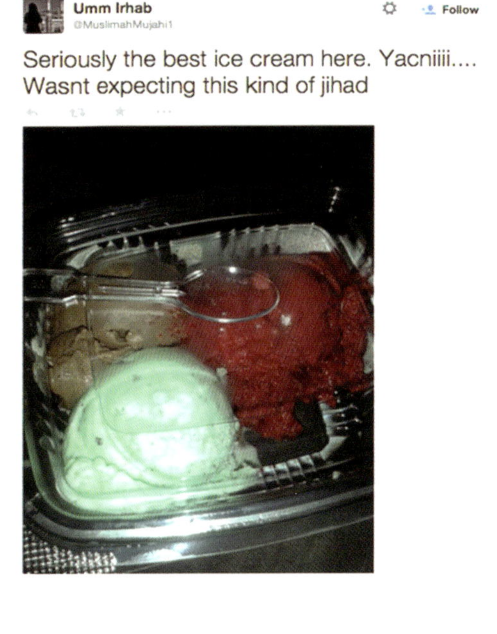

أبو العباس اللبناني
@Maxabbes
Follow

Believe it or not we even have cocktail in Raqqa , join in.

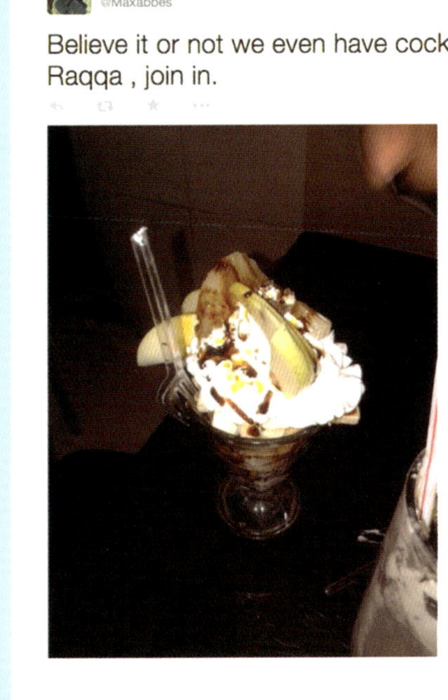

Britani
@Abuuthmaan1988
Following

There's more than just fighting here.

This is for those who love food.

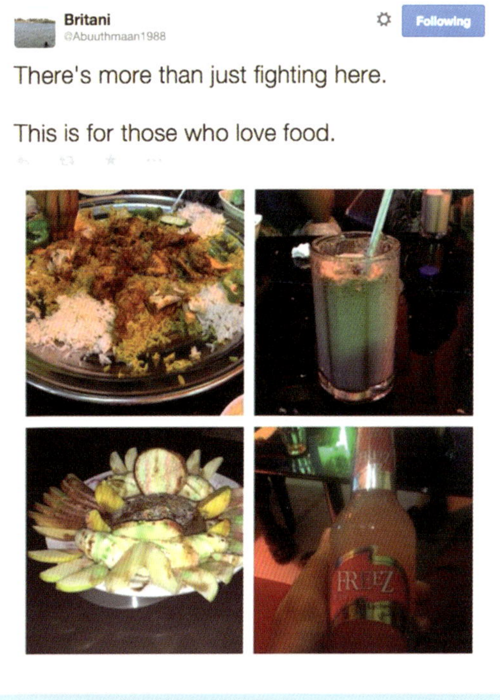

أبو العباس اللبناني
@Maxabbes

Dinner with the Brothers , join us.
Note : "I'm gonna keep sharing pics of food until you literally join us".

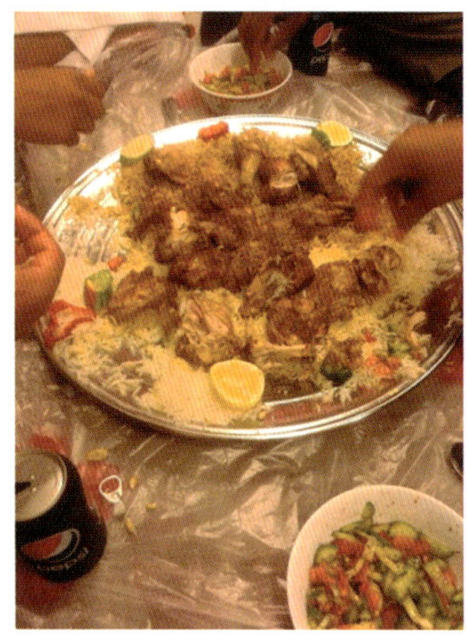

Noorman Al Fajr
@NoormanAlFajr

#Syria: Islamic State of Iraq and ash-Sham guys offer sweets and orange juice:

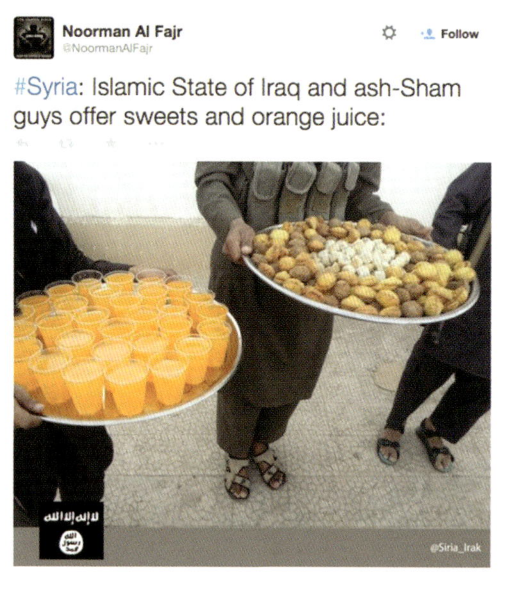

أبو العباس اللبناني
@Maxabbes

Brothers eating after fasting join us
Note: Anyone who mentions something about poor people somewhere will be blocked

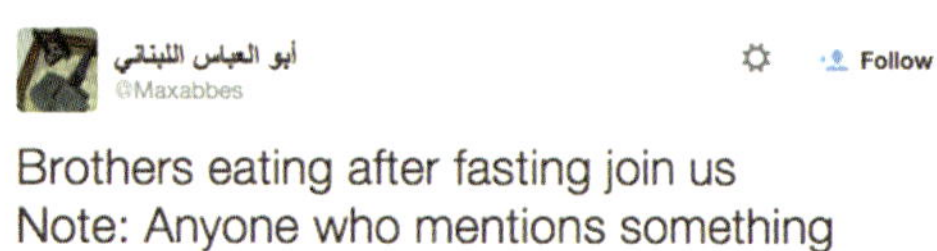

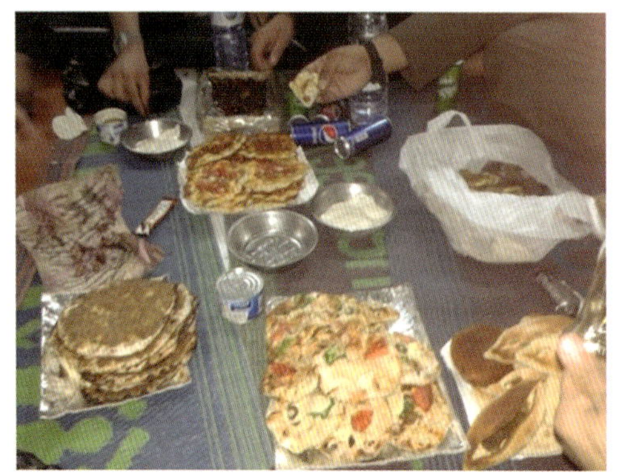

أبو العباس اللبناني
@Maxabbes

Fish from Euphrate river , delicious !

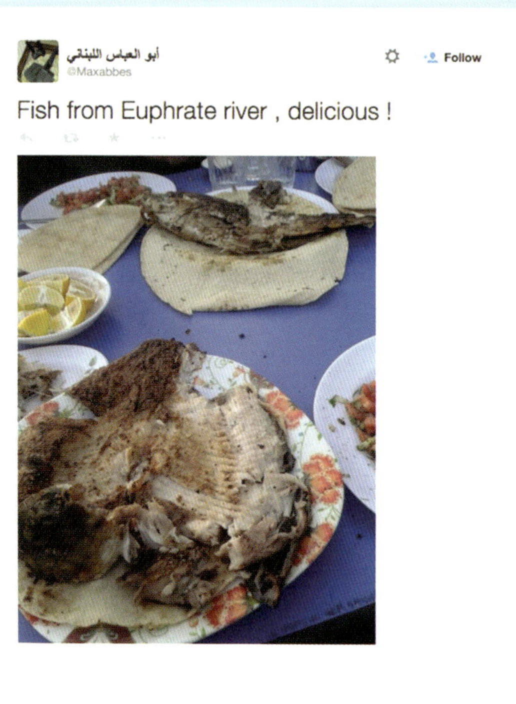

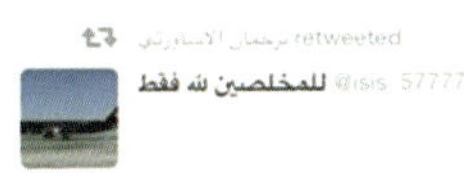

‏13 رحمان الأنصاري retweeted
للمخلصين لله فقط @isis 57777 · 17m
باذن الله سنحتفل بنصر عظيم
في معظم العراق والشام
وتتمدد باذن الله
الله اكبر
الله اكبر
ترقبوا اخبار سارة باذن الله

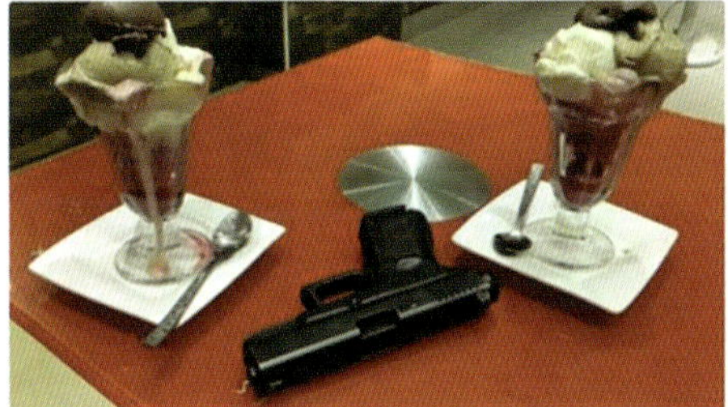

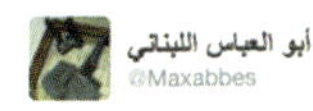

أبو العباس اللبناني
@Maxabbes
Follow
Having dinner with the brothers , join in .

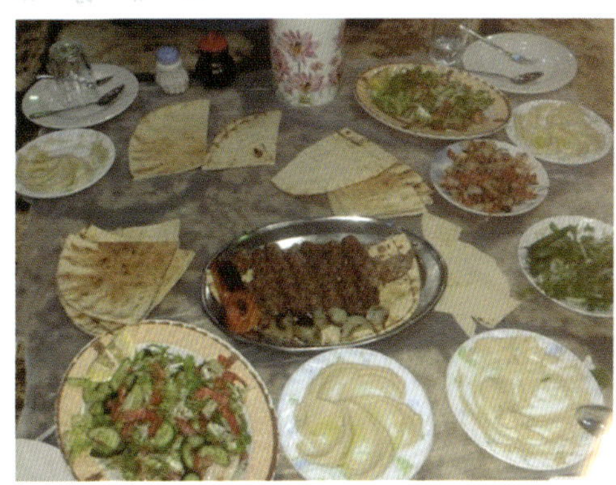

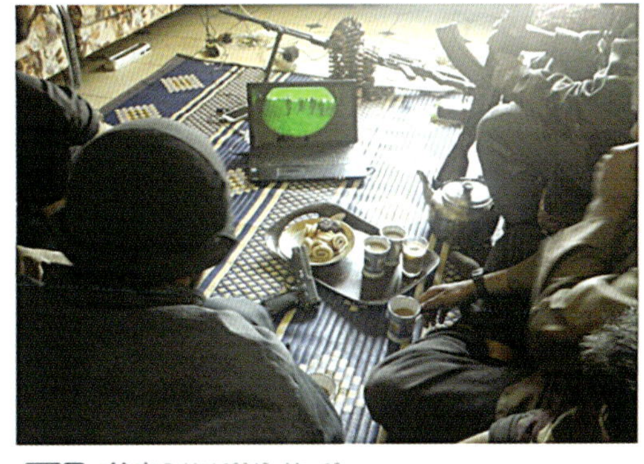

akhair @akhair12345 · May 19
@Dawla_NewsMedia Brothers on frontline enjoying cappaccino and cake while watching latest Saleel as-Swarem 4

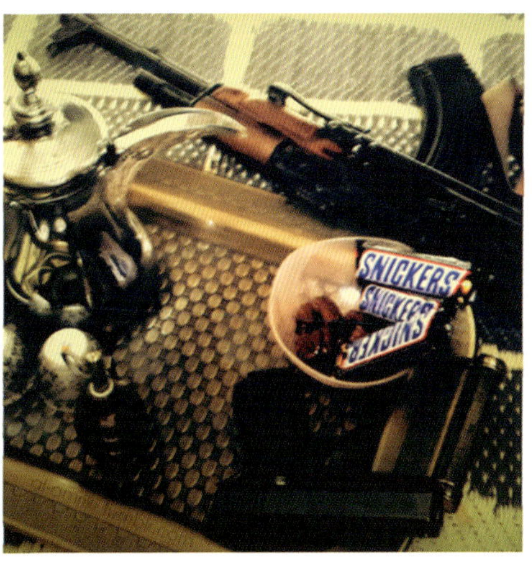

Islamic State Times @ISTimes2 · Oct 11
7. Most Muhajireen are extreme(ly) — in love with cats, kids, chocolate and other stuff. #IS
57   38

GOLD COAST

When Ying Ang was very young, she was a significant witness to a double murder and suicide attempt in her hometown.

She grew up in the Gold Coast, an Australian coastal city in southeastern Queensland, a place imagined and named by real estate investors and rife with contradictions. Though a major tourist destination, replete with surfing, theme parks, and nightclubs, the area is also widely known as Australia's crime capital.

In her latest body of photographs, simply titled *Gold Coast*, Yang confronts her childhood memories and the dark realities of her hometown, in a manner both sedate and reflective. The tonal power of her imagery might be found in a larger feeling of malaise in the modern western world. The onslaught of war, our rapidly degrading environment, the growing control of urban space by real estate investors, or the collapse of financial markets never quite succeed in resolving conflict or improving society. The western world lives in an era marked by apathy, a desire for normalcy, and even a denial of the looming changes in how we live.

Life in the Gold Coast is emblematic of this creeping ennui. Everything is neat, the houses are well kept, the sun is shining, the beaches are packed, and yet there is unease just below the surface. The inhabitants of the Gold Coast are trapped in a contradiction. According to Ying Ang, residents claim to live in a perfect place, but newspaper headlines proclaim the opposite.

Ang embraces the unresolved quasi-event. Her pictures document and penetrate the veneer of everyday life, never allowing the city's darkness to fully reveal itself. She treats the local architecture as a kind of urban theater—a trick intended to perpetuate the illusion of normalcy. BY NOAH RABINOWITZ

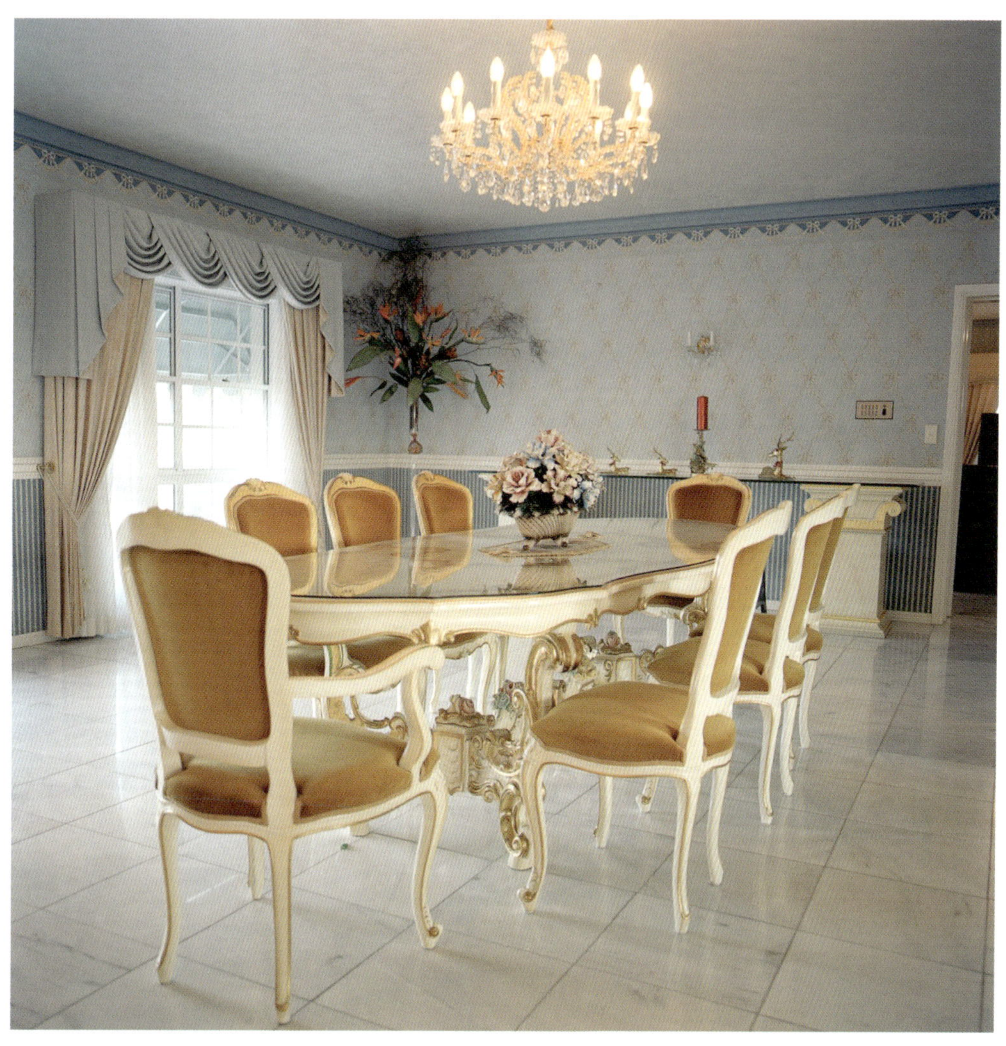

29 Cessnock Close (2013)

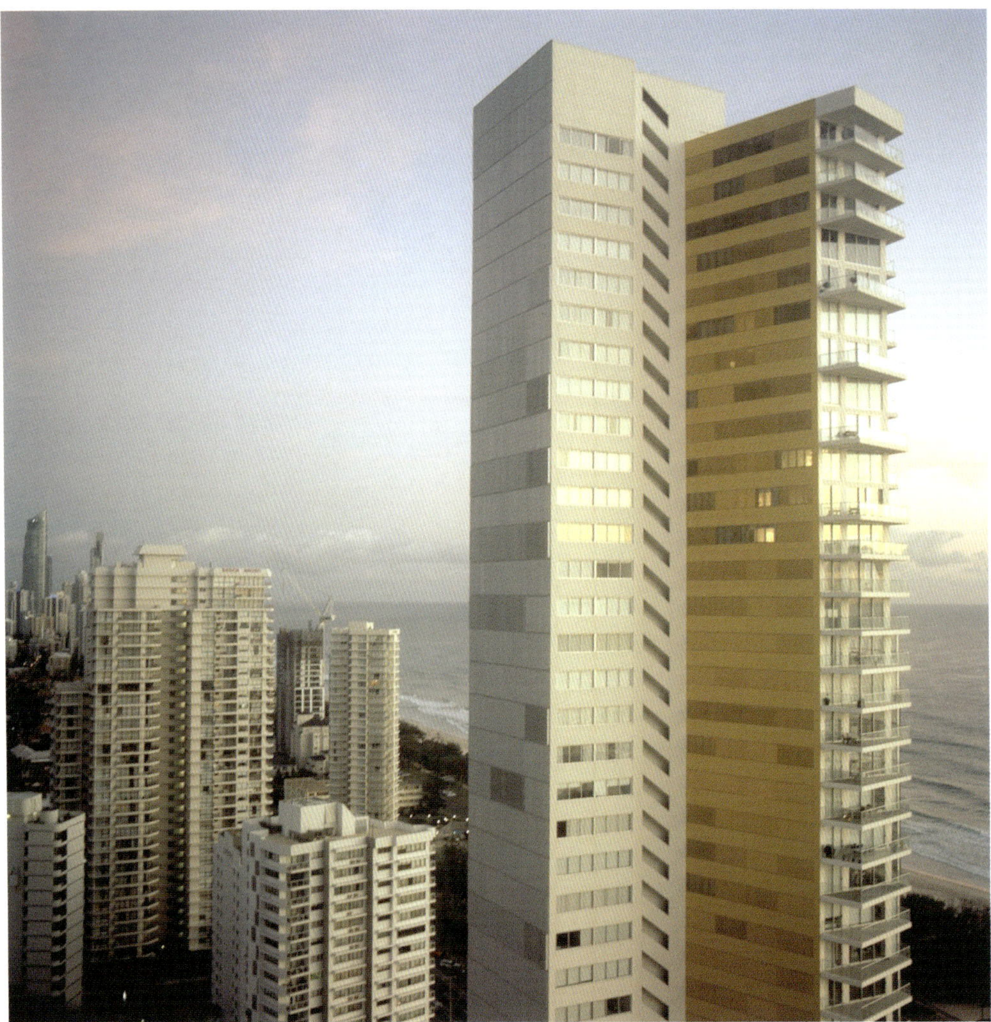

Broadbeach (2013)

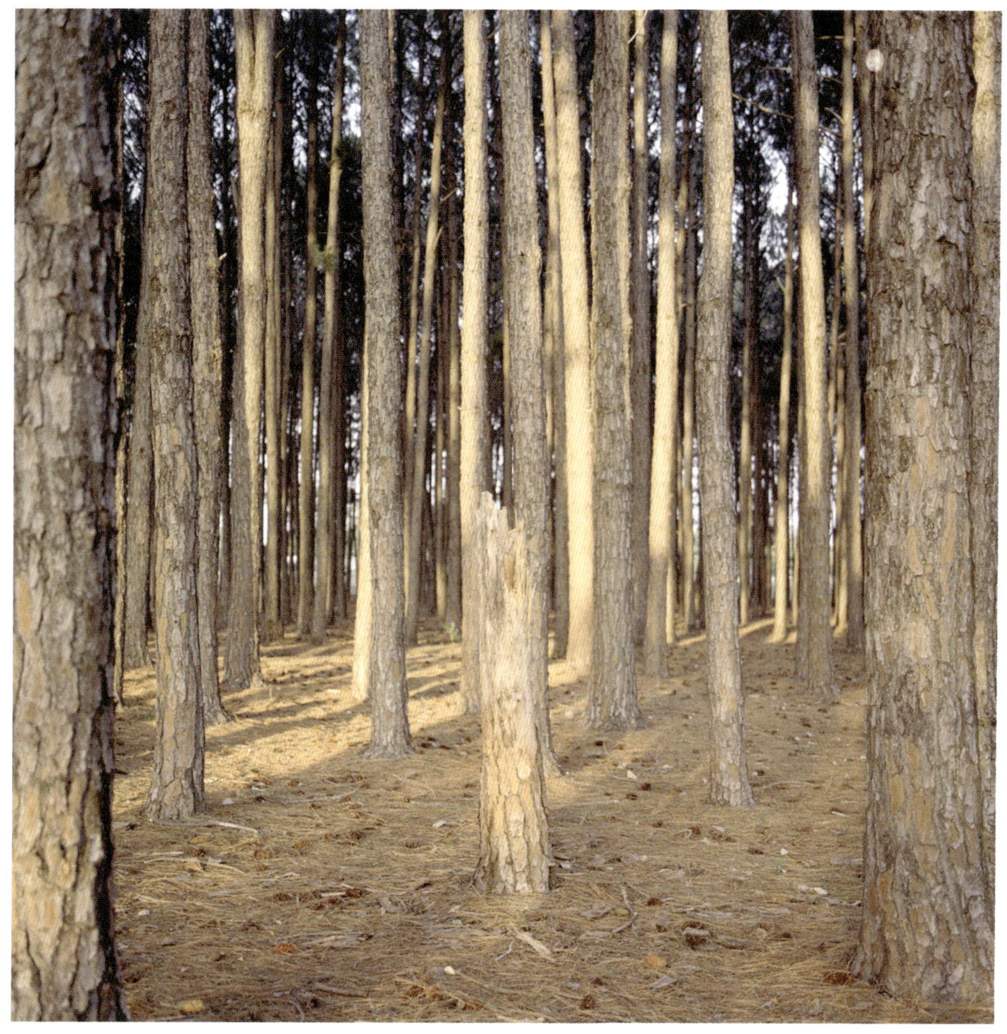

Behind Miami Grass Tennis Centre (2013)

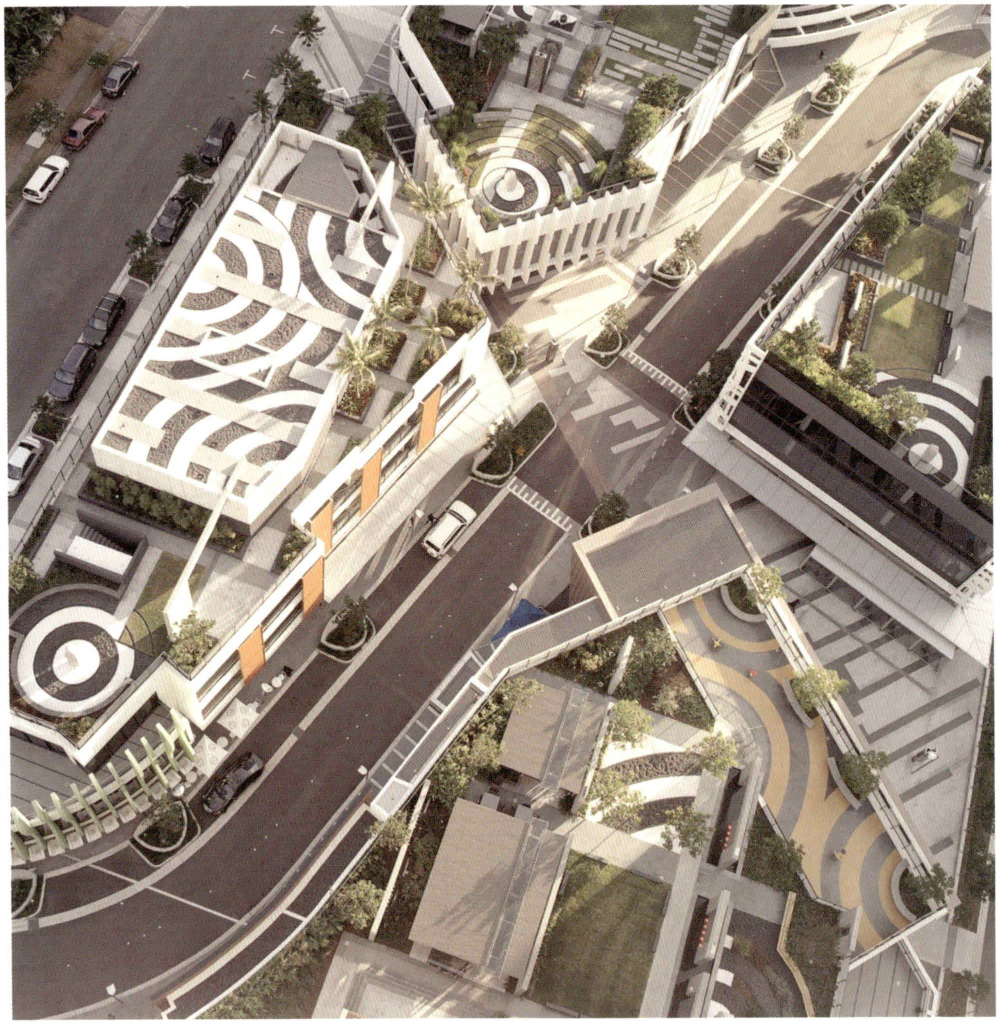

Surf Parade (2013)

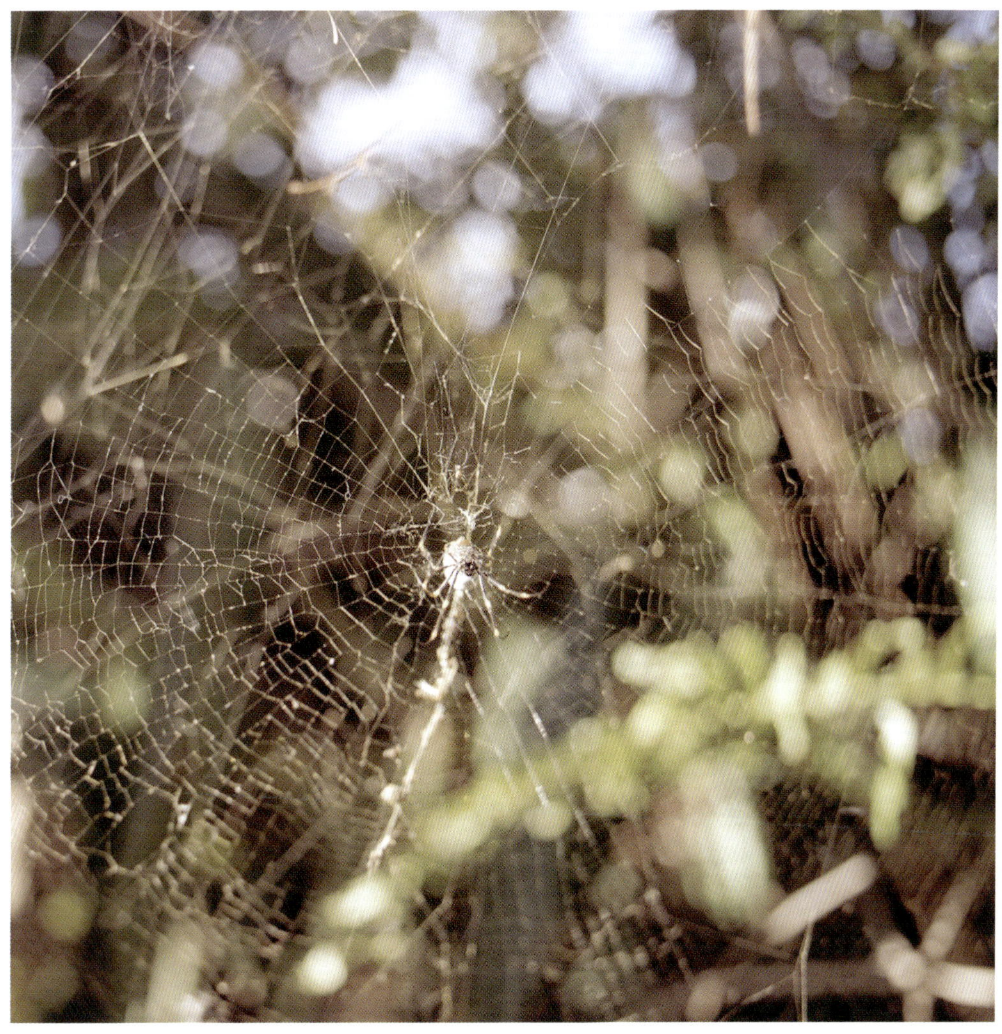

Sunday, 7am (2013)

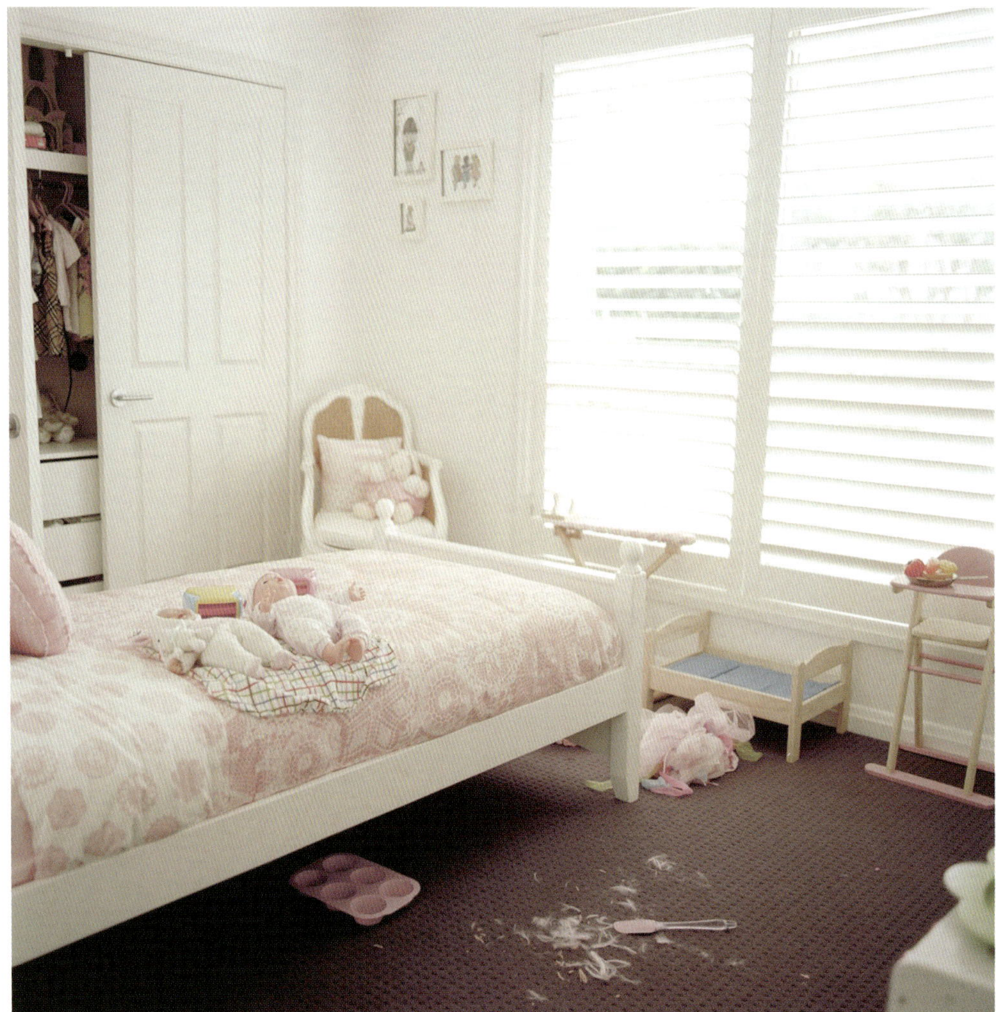

Wednesday March 6 (2013)

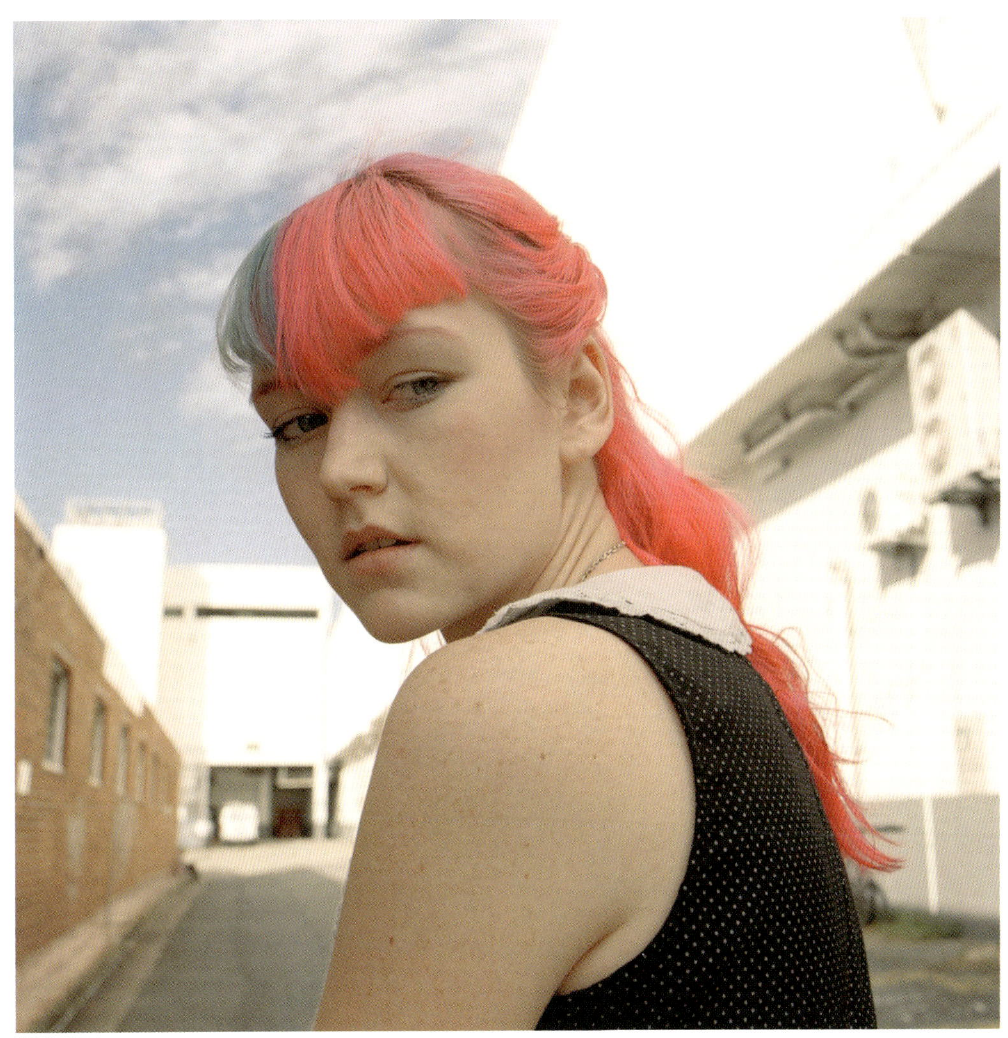

Australia Fair (2013)

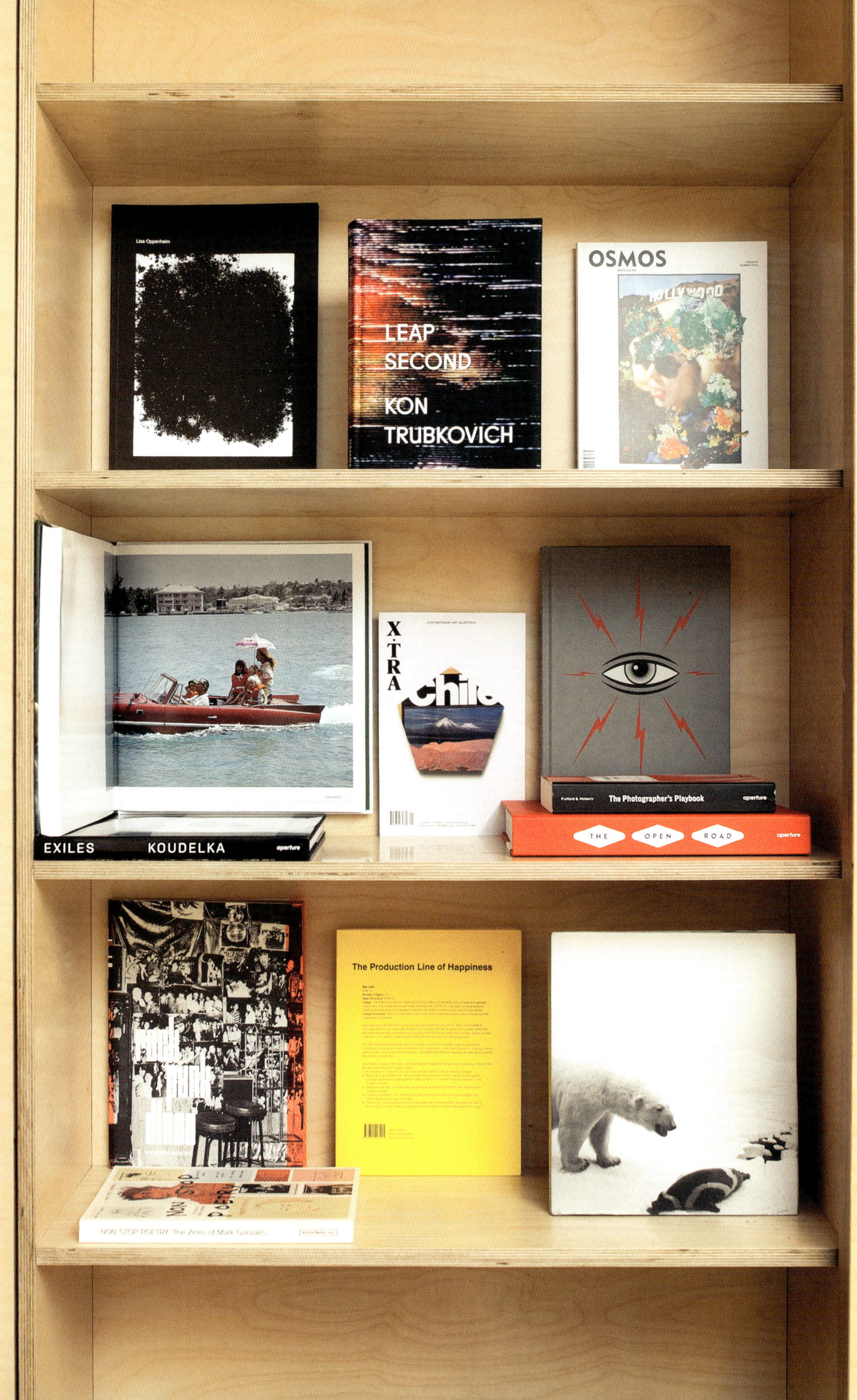

On Our Shelves

TOP

Lisa Oppenheim, Works 2003–2013, 159 pages, Sternberg Press, 2014

Kon Trubkovich: Leap Second, edited by Cay Sophie Rabinowitz, with texts by Nicolás Guagnini and Christian Rattemeyer, designed by Garrick Gott, 144 pages, OSMOS, 2014

OSMOS Magazine: Issue 04, 88 pages, OSMOS, 2014

MIDDLE

90 Degrees of Shade,100 Years of Photography in the Caribbean, edited by Stuart Baker, foreword by Paul Gilroy, 200 pages, Soul Jazz Books, 2014

Josef Koudelka: Exiles, texts by Czeslaw Milosz, Josef Koudelka, and Robert Delpire, 177 pages, Aperture, 2014

X-TRA Contemporary Art Quarterly, Vol. 17, no. 1, 221 pages, Project X Foundation for Art & Criticism, 2014

Ed Templeton: Wayward Cognitions, text by Stijn Huijts, 160 pages, Um Yeah Press, 2014

The Photographer's Playbook, edited by Jason Fulford and Gregory Halpern, 428 pages, Aperture, 2014

The Open Road: Photography and the American Roadtrip, edited by David Campany, 336 pages, Aperture, 2014

BOTTOM

Watanabe Katsumi: Rock Punk Disco, Photographs 1960s–1980s, designed by Garrick Gott, n.p., PPP Editions, 2014

Non Stop Poetry: The Zines of Mark Gonzales, edited by Philip Aarons and Emma Reeves, designed by Garrick Gott, 416 pages, Printed Matter Inc. 2014

Christopher Williams: The Production Line of Happiness, texts by Matthew S. Witkovsky, Mark Godfrey, and Roxana Marcoci, 166 pages, Art Institute of Chicago, Museum of Modern Art, and Yale University Press, 2014

Hiroshi Sugimoto, Unnatural Nature, 118 pages, Pace Gallery and Damiani, 2014

IS THIS ART?

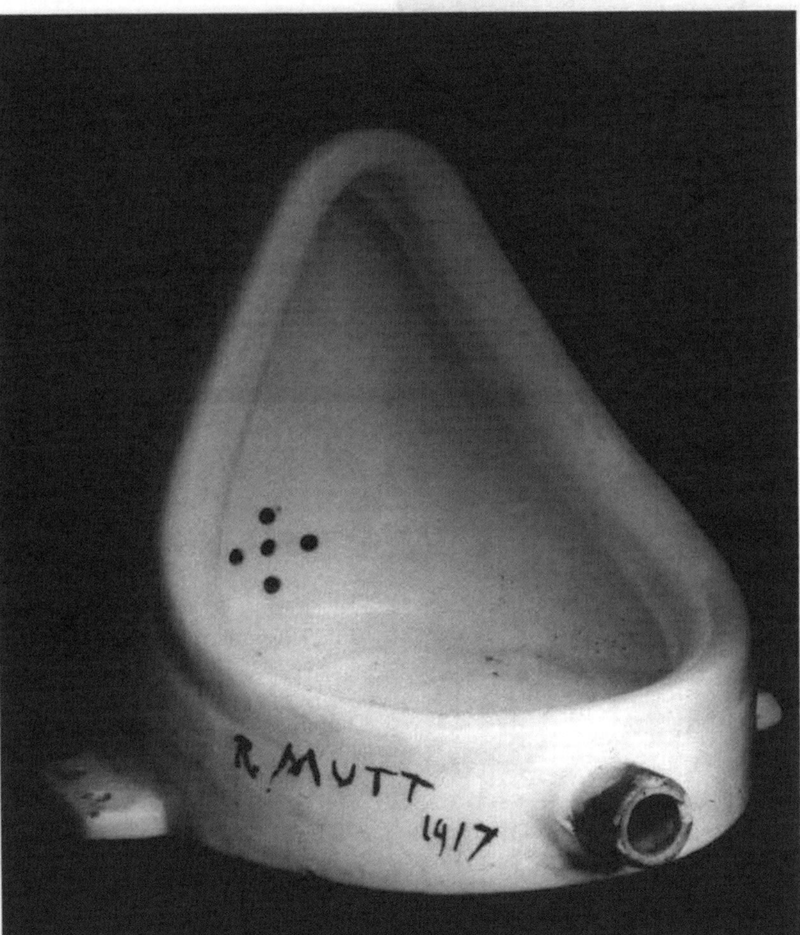

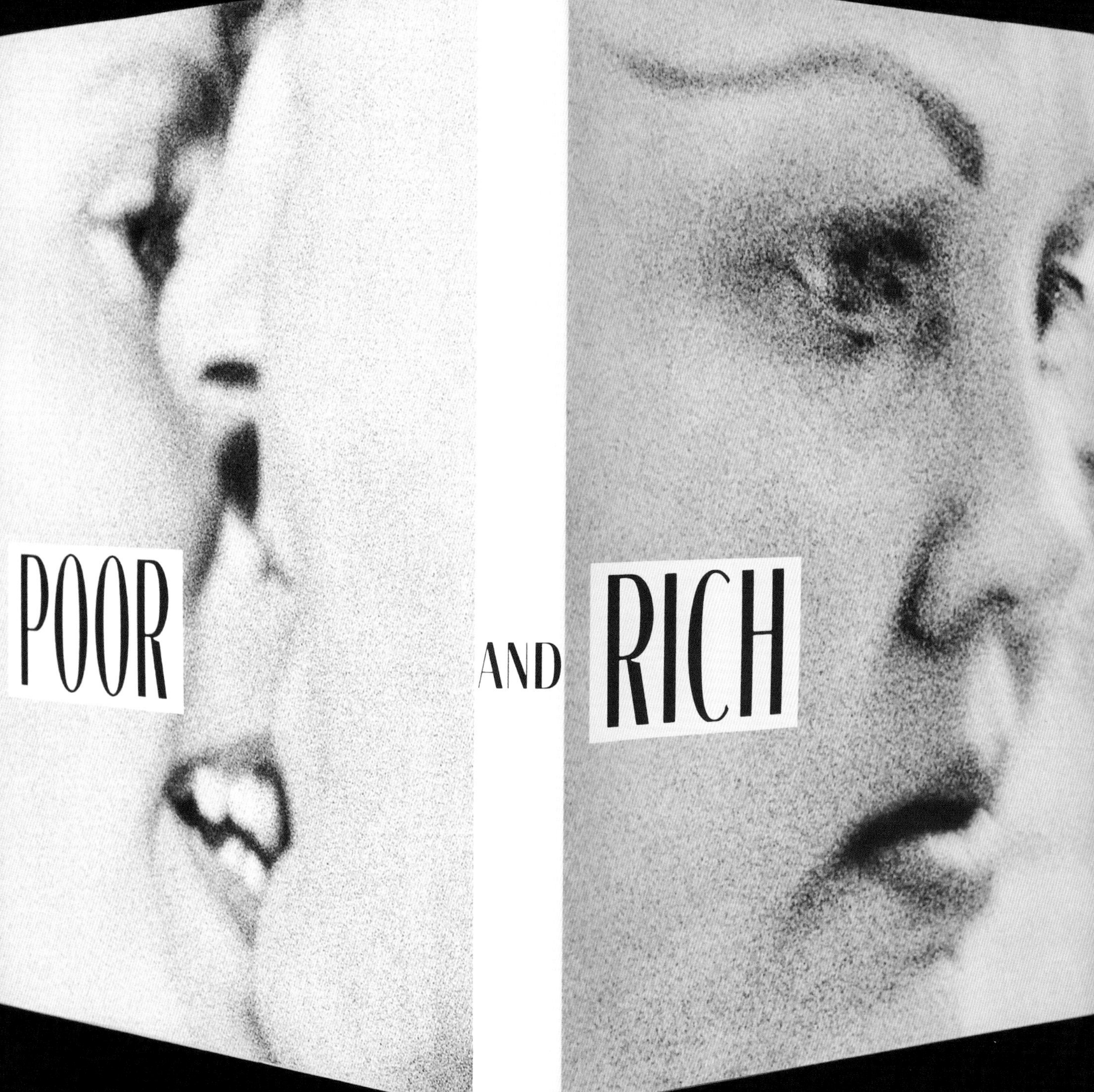
POOR
AND
RICH

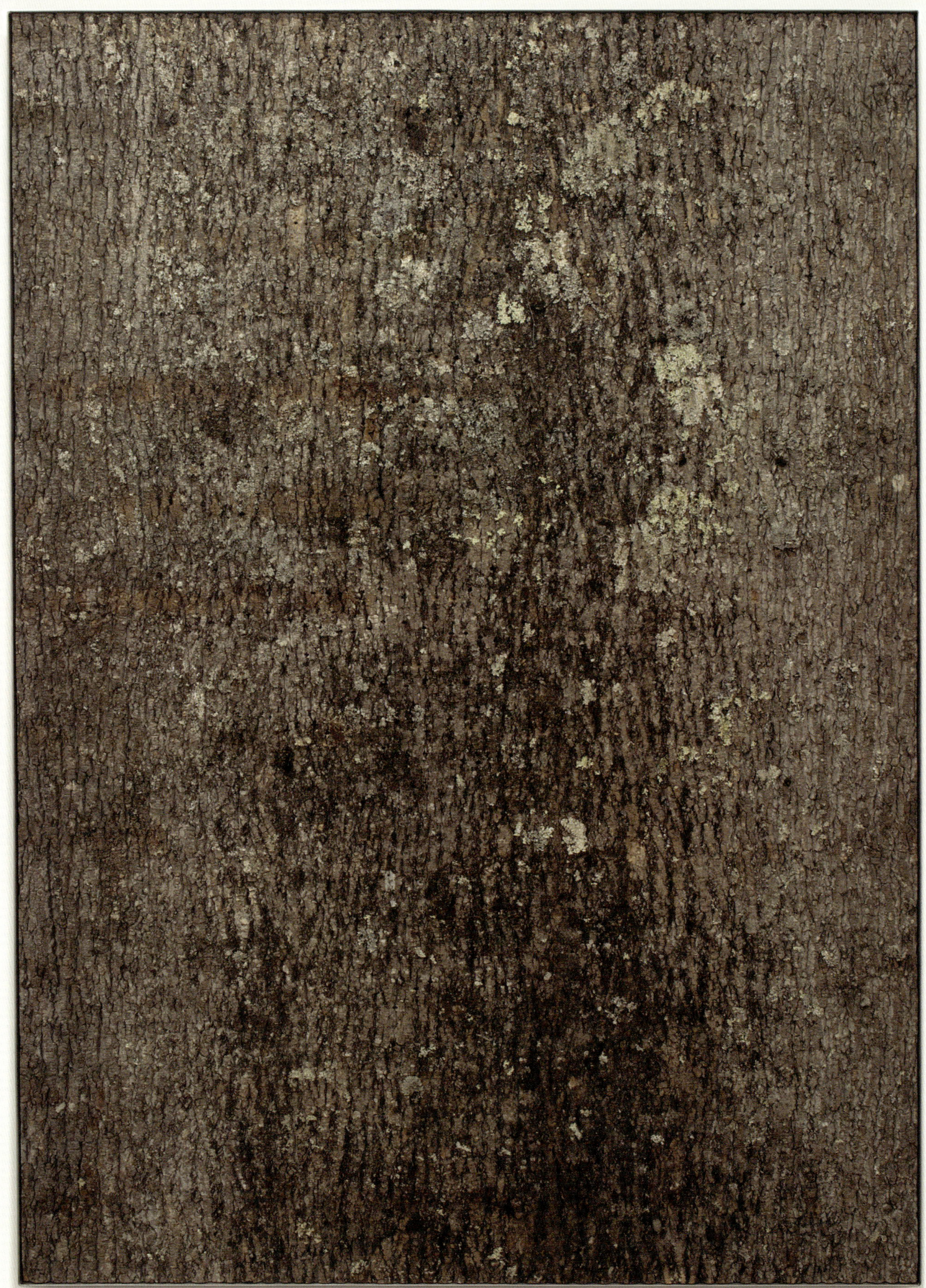

OHWOW

Nick van Woert, *Journey To The Surface Of The Earth (Boyle Family)*, 2014
Bark and stainless steel frame, 70.5 x 97 x 3 in. / 179 x 246.4 x 7.6 cm

www.oh-wow.com

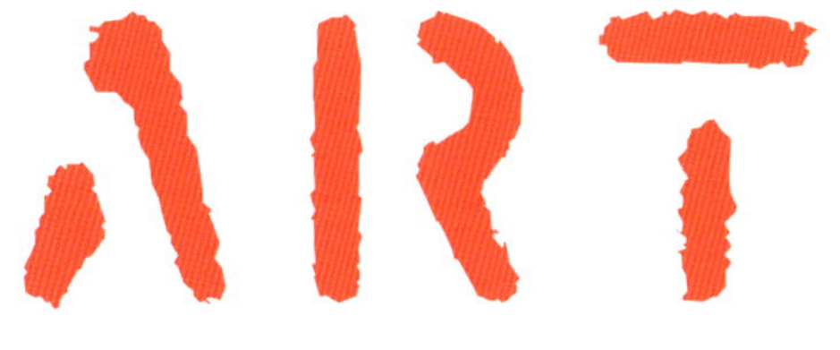

The Ebola crisis is far from over. Before the outbreak
Liberia had 51 doctors for 4 million people.
Many of them died. Rebuilding and reinforcing the
devastated health system of this country is critical
for a sustainable future and for the preparation
against future outbreaks of Ebola.

By owning a piece of art by one of these artists you are
supporting the ongoing work of LAST MILE HEALTH,
an organisation based in Liberia that trains local
health workers to respond to Ebola and distributes
medical supplies in difficult-to-reach areas.

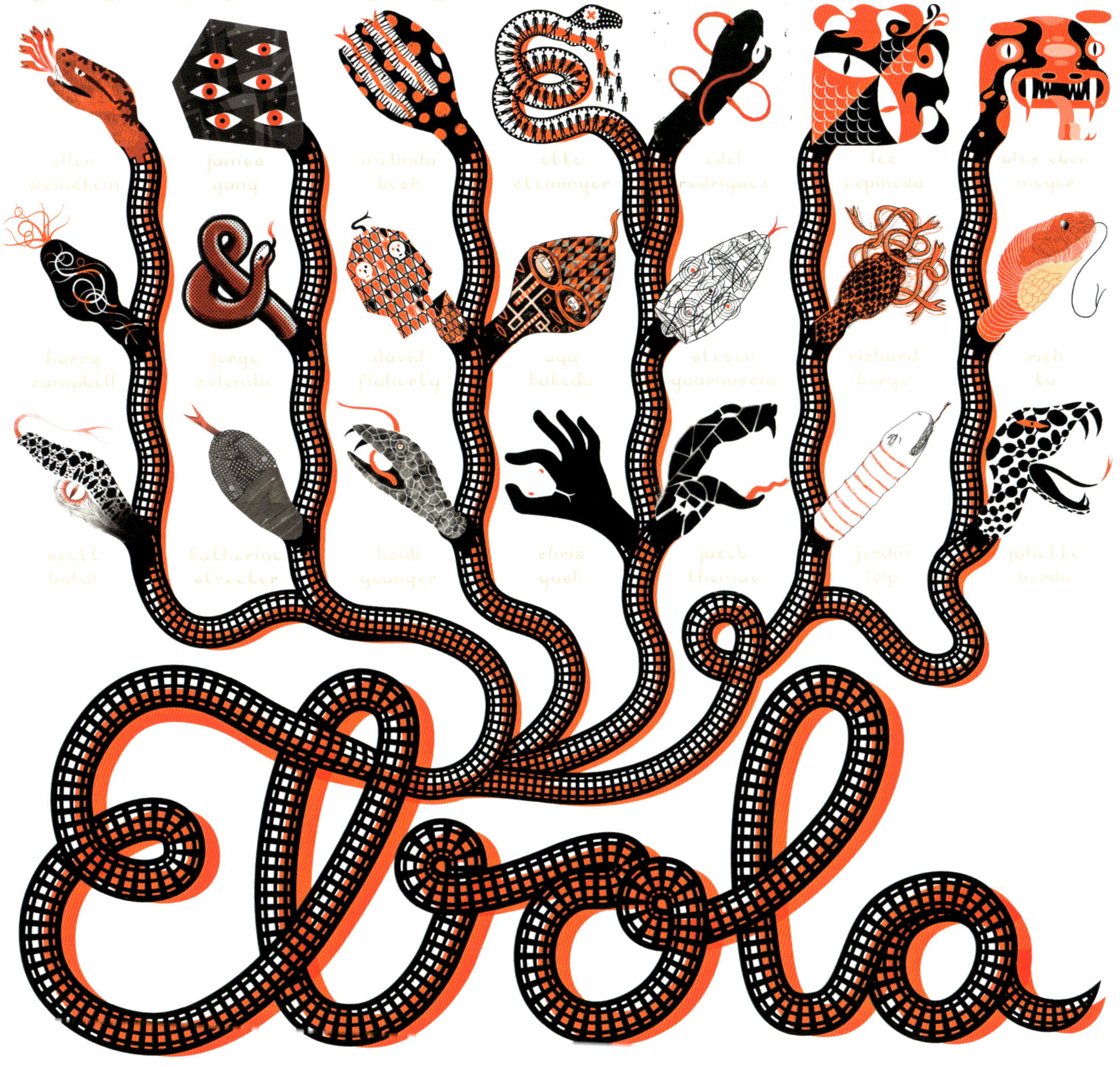

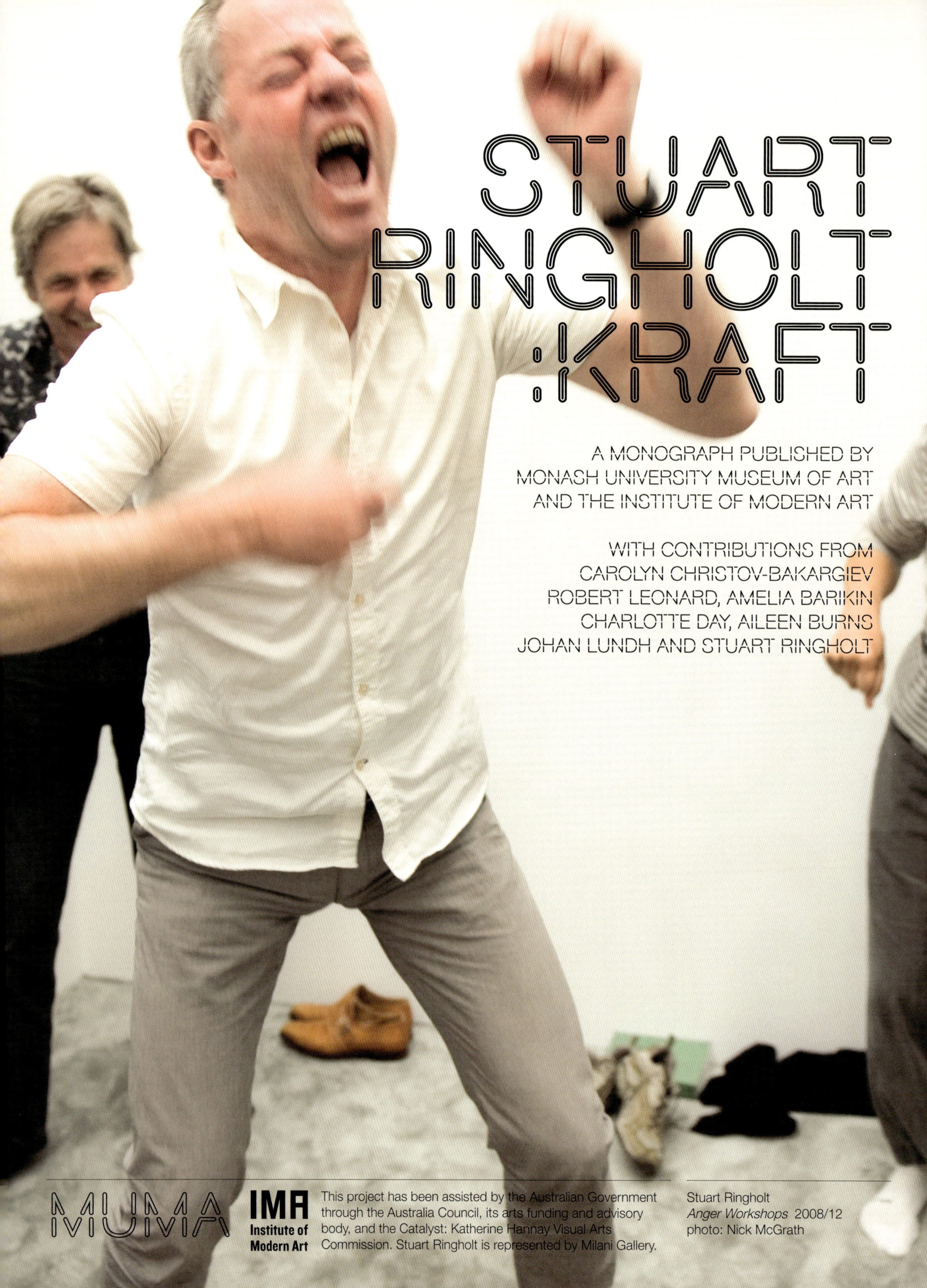
STUART
RINGHOLT
:KRAFT

A MONOGRAPH PUBLISHED BY
MONASH UNIVERSITY MUSEUM OF ART
AND THE INSTITUTE OF MODERN ART

WITH CONTRIBUTIONS FROM
CAROLYN CHRISTOV-BAKARGIEV
ROBERT LEONARD, AMELIA BARIKIN
CHARLOTTE DAY, AILEEN BURNS
JOHAN LUNDH AND STUART RINGHOLT

MUMA

IMA
Institute of
Modern Art

This project has been assisted by the Australian Government
through the Australia Council, its arts funding and advisory
body, and the Catalyst: Katherine Hannay Visual Arts
Commission. Stuart Ringholt is represented by Milani Gallery.

Stuart Ringholt
Anger Workshops 2008/12
photo: Nick McGrath

RICHARD ARTSCHWAGER
AT DAVID NOLAN GALLERY, NEW YORK
December 10, 2014 – January 31, 2015

The exhibition is accompanied by a comprehensive monograph on
Artschwager's landscape drawings with an essay by John Yau

Eva Artschwager at White Sands National Monument, New Mexico © Richard Artschwager, courtesy Ann Artschwager

DAVID NOLAN NEW YORK

527 West 29th Street New York NY 10001   Tel: +1 212 925 6190   www.davidnolangallery.com

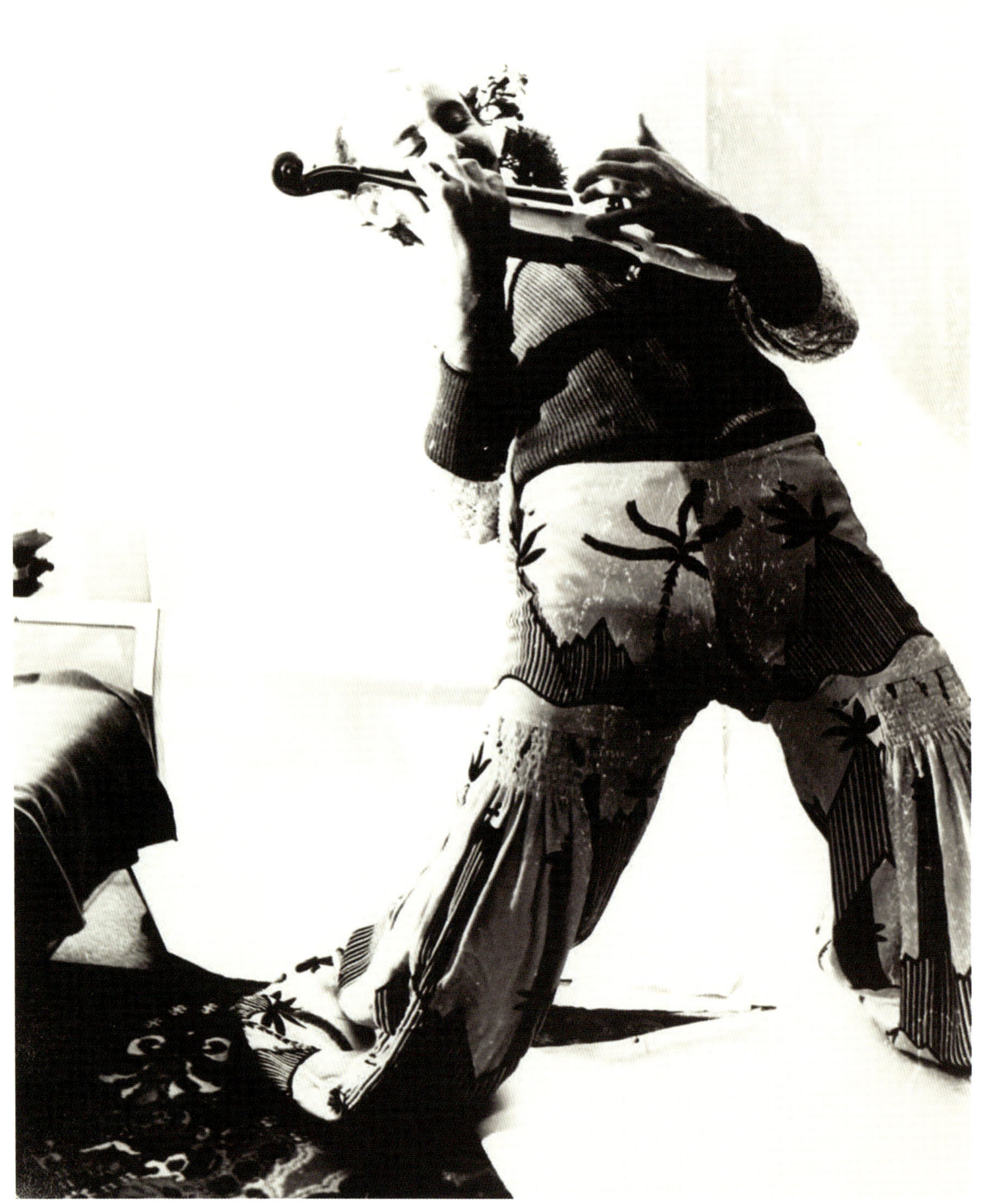

SIGMAR POLKE

THE DISTANCE TO THINGS – THE PROXIMITY TO THINGS
PHOTOGRAPHS AND DRAWINGS FROM THE 60S AND 70S, THE VOGEL COLLECTION
THROUGH DECEMBER 23 · 297 TENTH AVENUE NEW YORK 10001

PAULKASMINGALLERY.COM

Untitled (Playing music in the Kirchfeldstr.), 1970-71, silver gelatin print, 9½ x 7 in. / 24 x 18 cm © The Estate of Sigmar Polke / ARS, New York

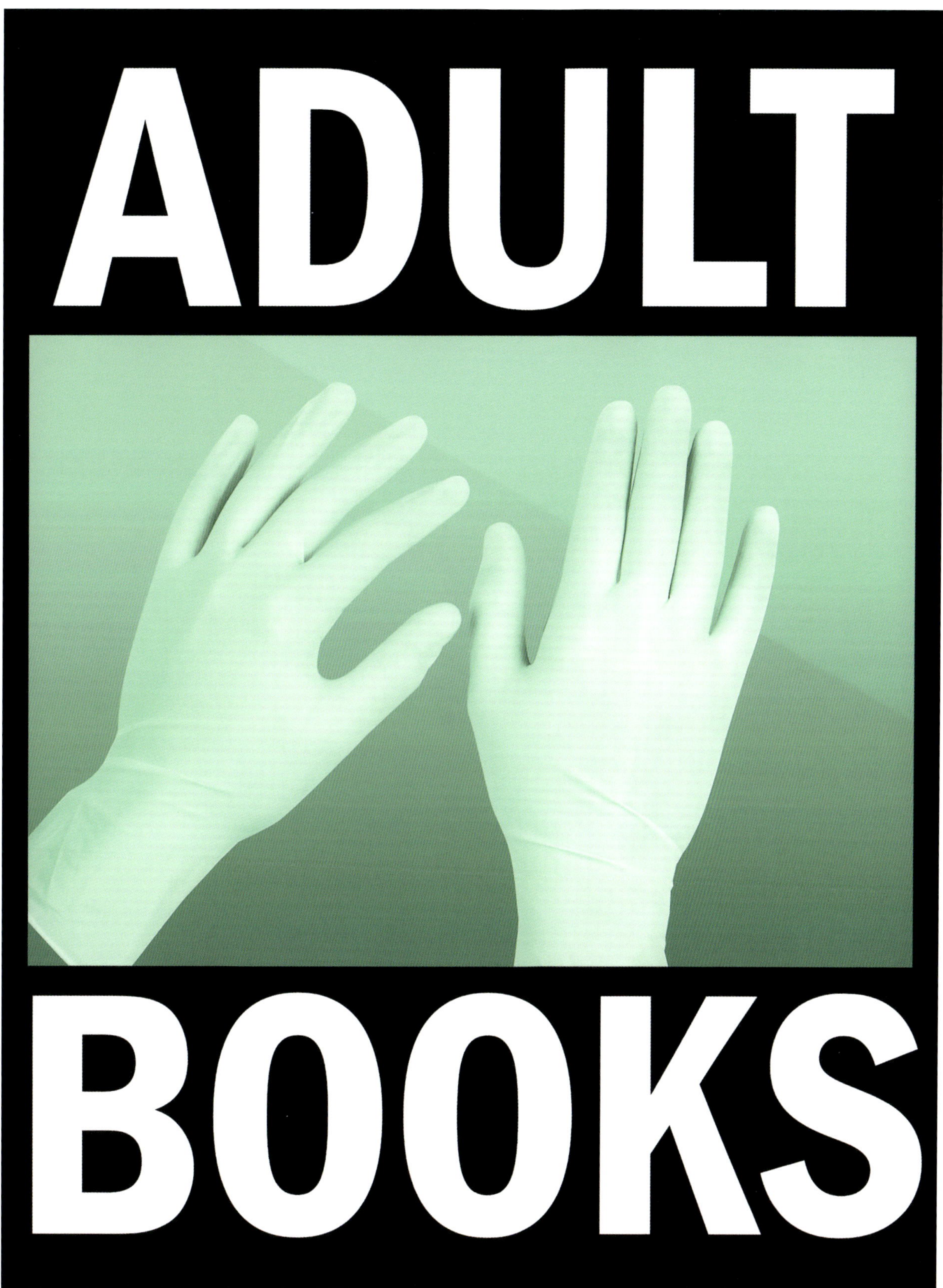

LA Art Book Fair 2015 Fundraising Edition by Cali Thornhill Dewitt

Printed Matter, Inc.

Credits

Essay: Keiichi Tanaami

Collage Book 1_07 (1971)
Ink, marker, collage on
paper
11.75 x 14.75 in

Collage Book 7_13 (1971)
Ink, marker, collage on
paper
15.375 x 17.75 in

Collage Book 7_50 (1970)
Ink, marker, collage on
paper
15.375 x 17.75 in

Collage Book 9_10 (1971)
Ink, marker, collage on
paper
19.25 x 21.25 in

42nd Street Scissors
(1969)
Ink on paper
15.25 x 18.875 in

42nd Street Letter (c. late
1960s)
Ink, old magazine scraps,
collage on paper
15.125 x 18.875 in

All images courtesy of
Sikkema Jenkins & Co.

**Story:
Mohamed Bourouissa**

Running Slave (2014)
Color photograph

It's for the kid (2013)
Color photograph

Sans Titre (2014)
Pencil and collaged ink jet
print on paper

Skin and paper (2014)
Color photograph

Pegasus (2014)
Color photograph

Sans Titre (2014)
Pencil and collaged ink jet
print on paper

Horse Day (2014)
Film still

Horse Day (2014)
Film still

All images © 2014
Mohamed Bourouissa
Courtesy the artist and
Kamel Menour, Paris

**Eye of the Beholder:
William Copley**

Titles refer to paintings
pictured in the photographs:

Iris Jouante (1961)
Oil on canvas with sand

Lily Niagra No. 2 (1962)
Oil on canvas

Persephone (1960)
Oil on canvas

Cafe du Bon B (1960)
Oil on canvas

*Model for English
Flag* (1961)
Oil on canvas

Jigsaw Puzzle (1957)
Oil on canvas

Pharmacie (1958)
Oil on canvas

All images courtesy of
William N. Copley Estate
and Paul Kasmin Gallery

**Picture Perfect:
Wardell Milan**

Lovely tulip #7 (2012)
Charcoal, oil, oil pastel,
crayon on paper
44 x 30 in

Lovely tulip #2 (2012)
Charcoal, oil, oil pastel,
crayon on paper
22 x 30 in

*Late afternoon, between
late summer and early fall
#1* (2013)
Oil pastel, charcoal, pastel,
ink on paper
58 x 60

*Sunday, sitting on the bank
of Butterfly Meadow*
(2013)
Photograph
40 x 60 in

Exotic Perfume (vivica)
(2013)
Collage, oil pastel on
magazine page
11.5 x 16.5 in

Exotic Perfume (Hollywood)
(2013)
Oil paint chips on magazine
page
11.5 x 16.5 in

All images courtesy of
the artist and David Nolan
Gallery

**Portfolio:
Tamara Rafkin**

Sleeping Houses 6
(2007)
C-print photograph
30 x 30 in

Sleeping Houses 18
(2012)
C-print photograph
30 x 30 in

Sleeping Houses 13
(2009)
C-print photograph
30 x 30 in

Sleeping Houses 14
(2007)
C-print photograph
30 x 30 in

Sleeping Houses 19
(2012)
C-print photograph
30 x 30 in

Watchful Houses 1 (2013)
C-Print Photograph
30 x 30 in

Watchful Houses 2 (2013)
C-print photograph
30 x 30 in

Watchful Houses 20
(2014)
C-print photograph
30 x 30 in

Watchful Houses 4 (2013)
C-print photograph
30 x 30 in

All images courtesy of the
artist

**Means to an End:
Edward Steichen**

*Sugar Cubes: Design for
Stehli Silk Corporation*
(1926–1927)
Gelatin silver print
Bequest of Edward
Steichen under
the direction of
Joanna T. Steichen,
1979:2421:0002
Courtesy of George
Eastman House,
International Museum of
Photography and Film

*Cigarettes and Matches:
Design for Stehli Silk
Corporation* (1926–1927)
Gelatin silver print
Bequest of Edward
Steichen under
the direction of
Joanna T. Steichen,

1979:2421:0001
Courtesy of George
Eastman House,
International Museum of
Photography and Film

*Tacks: Design for Stehli Silk
Corporation* (1926)
Gelatin silver print, printed
later
Bequest of Edward
Steichen under
the direction of
Joanna T. Steichen,
1979:2421:0011
Courtesy of George
Eastman House,
International Museum of
Photography and Film

Beans Stehli Silk Design
(c. 1927)
Printed silk fabric
16.5625 x 9.25 in
Gift of the photographer.
Edward Steichen Archive,
II.C.7*.
The Museum of Modern
Art Archives, New York,
ARCH.140

Rice Stehli Silk Design (c.
1927)
Printed silk fabric
16.75 x 7.625 in
Gift of the photographer.
Edward Steichen Archive,
II.C.7*.
The Museum of Modern
Art Archives, New York,
ARCH.141

Steichen Endnotes

1: Marguerite Tazelaar,
"Portrait of a Pioneer,"
Movie Makers, July 1927.
Edward Steichen Archive,
II.C.2. The Museum of
Modern Art Archives, New
York.
2: Marguerite Tazelaar,
"Portrait of a Pioneer,"
Movie Makers, July 1927.
Edward Steichen Archive,
II.C.2. The Museum of
Modern Art Archives, New
York.

**Still Moving Still:
Colin Snapp**

All images are stills from:

NV Regional (2013)
Single-channel anamorphic
digital video
90 min

All images courtesy of the
artist and Galerie Allen,
Paris

**Sample Size:
Andrea Arrubla**

Lovesick Drawing 10
(2014)
Chalk and marker on
Newspaper
16.5 x 19.75 in

Lovesick Drawing 4 (2014)
Chalk and marker on
Newspaper
20 x 27.5 in

Lovesick Drawing 3 (2014)
Chalk and marker on
Newspaper
10 x 13.75 in

Lovesick Drawing 1 (2014)
Chalk and marker on
Newspaper
10 x 13.75 in

All images courtesy of the
artist

Portfolio: Jiři Thýn

All works are from
the ongoing series
*Basic Study/Narrative
Photography*

*Consciousness as a
Fundamental Attribute II*
(2014). *frieze, October
2013, issue 158, p. 212*
Black and white
photograph on baryta
paper
Dimensions variable

*Consciousness as a
Fundamental Attribute II*
(2014). *frieze, October
2013, issue 158*
Color photograph
Dimensions variable

*Consciousness as a
Fundamental Attribute I*
(2013)
Slide show still
Black and white 35mm
photograph transferred to
digital video
*Consciousness as a
Fundamental Attribute II*
(2014). *frieze, October
2013, issue 158*
Color photograph
Dimensions variable

*Consciousness as a
Fundamental Attribute II*
(2014). *frieze, October
2013, Issue 158, p. 241*
Black and white
photograph on baryta
paper
Dimensions variable

*Consciousness as a
Fundamental Attribute II*
(2014). *frieze, October
2013, Issue 158*
Black and white
photograph on baryta
paper
Dimensions variable

All works courtesy of the
artist and hunt kastner
gallery, Prague

Reportage: Ying Ang

29 Cessnock Close (2013)
Archival inkjet print

Broadbeach (2013)
Archival inkjet print

*Behind Miami Grass Tennis
Centre* (2013)
Archival inkjet print

Surf Parade (2013)
Archival inkjet print

Sunday, 7 am (2013)
Archival inkjet print

Wednesday March 6
(2013)
Archival inkjet print

Australia Fair (2013)
Archival inkjet print

All images courtesy of the
artist

Contributors

Ying Ang is a photographer of social and contemporary issues based in Melbourne and New York City. Her interests lie in creating visual and literary content for print, web, and installation, exploring a range of formats and styles. She attended The International Centre of Photography after pursuing post-graduate studies in political science.

Isolde Brielmaier is the Director of the Contemporary Art Initiative at Westfield World Trade Center, in New York City. She is an Adjunct Professor at New York University and has curated, programmed, and written extensively on contemporary art and culture. Previously, Brielmaier has worked for the Guggenheim Museum, the Bronx Museum of Art, and as Chief Curator for the SCAD Museum of Art, in Savannah, Georgia. She holds a PhD from Columbia University.

Leon Dische Becker is a writer, editor, and translator born in Berlin, Germany. He currently lives between New York and Los Angeles.

Tom McDonough is a critic, art historian, and writer whose work ranges from the history of the European avant-gardes to the examination of contemporary artistic practices. He is the author of *The Beautiful Language of My Century* (2007), a study of radicalism in postwar French culture. His most recent book is the anthology *The Situationists and the City* (2009). McDonough is associate professor and chair of the Art History department at Binghamton University.

Ann Marie Peña is Associate Director of Frith Street Gallery in London. She has taught Visual Studies at the University of the Arts London, and in 2011 initiated the Artist in Residence program at the Art Gallery of Ontario in Toronto, where she curated an ambitious program of international artists that included Mohamed Bourouissa.

Brian Sholis is Associate Curator of Photography at the Cincinnati Art Museum. He wishes to acknowledge the scholarship on Steichen's commercial work by Patricia A. Johnston.

Colin Snapp was born and raised on Lopez Island WA. He received a BFA in filmmaking from the San Francisco Art Institute (2006). Recent solo exhibitions include *National Charter* (2013) at The Journal Gallery in Brooklyn, *IRND* (2014) at Galerie Allen in Paris, and *Deluxe Automatic* (2014) at Ibid Projects in London. His monograph *VISTA* was published by Études Studio (2013). Currently, Snapp is working on two feature-length films that focus on the psychology of the mediated experience within the American National Park System. He lives and works in New York, NY

Colophon

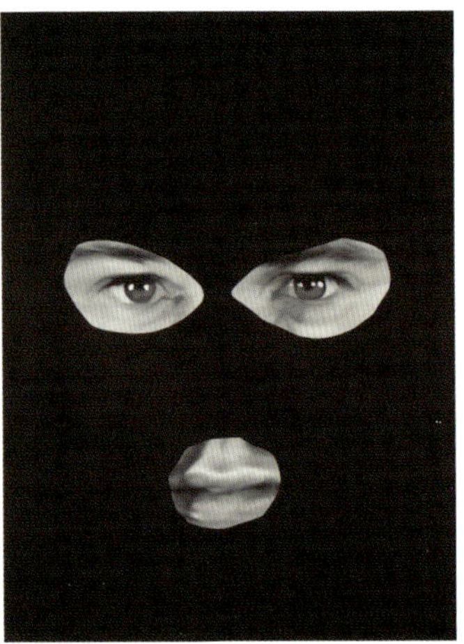

The Cover
Michael St. John
Visage (2010)
Oil on canvas
48 x 36 in

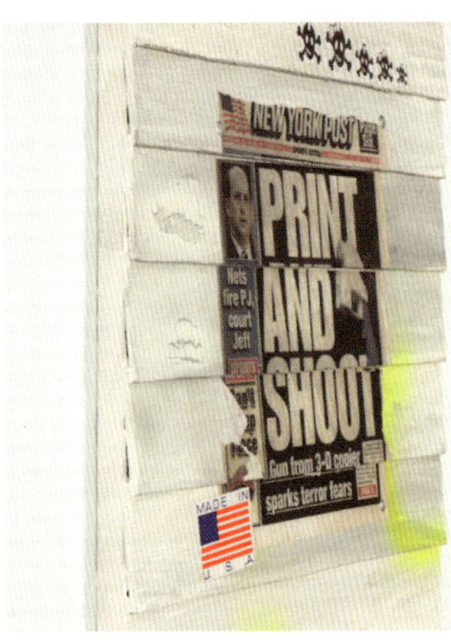

The Back Cover
Michael St. John
Guns (2014)
Collage and acrylic on wood
19 x 19 x 1 in

Images courtesy of Andrea Rosen Gallery

As always, the cover story will appear in the next issue.

Editor-in-Chief
Cay Sophie Rabinowitz

Associate Editor
Noah Rabinowitz

Copy Editor
Eugenia Bell

Editorial Assistant
Liz Pasqualo

Creative Director
Christian Rattemeyer

Art Director
Joshua Shaddock

Contributing Editors
Arianne Di Nardo
Thomas McDonough
Carter Mull
Emma Reeves
Sam Samore
Troy Selvaratnam

Published By
OSMOS
50 East 1st Street
New York, NY 10003

Subscriptions
OSMOS Magazine
50 East 1st Street
New York, NY 10003
osmos.assistant@gmail.com
T + 1 917 859 7104

Distribution
North America:
D.A.P/ Distributed
Arts Publishers
155 6th Avenue, 2nd FL
New York, NY 10013
www.artbook.com

Printer
Printed in the USA
by Drew & Rogers, Inc.

Paper
120lb. Endurance silk cover
100lb. Endurance silk text

Thanks to
Saadane Afif, Joseph Allen, Brian Anderson, Ying Ang, Andrea Arrubla, Lucien Bahaj, Zac Bahaj, Fiona Banner, Jonathan Bender, Aaron Bondaroff, Stefania Bortolami, Maureen Bray, Isolde Brielmaier, Lance Brewer, Luke Brown, Teresa Burk, Priscilla Caldwell, Shannon Michael Cane, Mehdi Chouakri, Liz Deschenes, Leon Dische Becker, Michelle Elligott, David Fierman, Yvonne Force-Villareal, Casey Fremont, Alexie Glass, Mark Godfrey, Garrick Gott, Alvin Hall, Martin Hatebur, Frank Hornig, Paul Kasmin, Charlotta Kotik, Casey Legler, Amanda Love, Justin Luke, George Newall, Mark Markin, Sarah Hermanson Meister, Duane Michals, Wardell Milan, Josh Milani, Al Moran, Mills Moran, Jordan Nassar, Michelle Newton, David Nolan, Cory Nomura, Nicholas Onley, Marcelo Krasilcic, Eric Kroll, Ann Marie Pena, Ralph Rabinowitz, Tamara Rafkin, Katie Rashid, Volker Rattemeyer, Michal Raz-Russo, Doreen Remen, Cory Reynolds, Stuart Ringholt, Andrea Rosen, Adriano Sack, Brian Sholis, Brent Sikkema, Michael St. John, Jiří Thýn, Kon Trubkovich, Philip Vanderhyden, Danh Vo, Bennett Williams, Matthew Wittkovsky